Fine WoodWorking | Best Workbenches

From the **Editors of** *Fine Woodworking*

 The Taunton Press

The Taunton Press
Inspiration for hands-on living®

THE TAUNTON PRESS, INC.
63 South Main Street, PO Box 5506
Newtown, CT 06470-5506
e-mail: tp@taunton.com

EDITOR: Jessica DiDonato
COPY EDITOR: Seth Reichgott
INDEXER: Jay Kreider
COVER & INTERIOR DESIGN: Carol Singer
LAYOUT: Laura Lind Design

LIBRARY OF CONGRESS CATALOGING-IN-PUBLICATION DATA

Fine woodworking best workbenches / editors of Fine Woodworking.
      p. cm.
   Includes index.
   ISBN 978-1-60085-389-0
   1. Workbenches. I. Taunton Press. II. Taunton's fine woodworking. III. Title: Best workbenches.
   TT197.5.W6F56 2012
   684.08--dc23
                        2011039812

PRINTED IN THE UNITED STATES OF AMERICA
10 9 8 7 6 5 4 3 2 1

ABOUT YOUR SAFETY: Working wood is inherently dangerous.
Using hand or power tools improperly or ignoring safety practices can lead
to permanent injury or even death. Don't try to perform operations you
learn about here (or elsewhere) unless you're certain they are safe for you.
If something about an operation doesn't feel right, don't do it. Look for
another way. We want you to enjoy the craft, so please keep safety foremost
in your mind whenever you're in the shop.

ACKNOWLEDGMENTS

Special thanks to the authors, editors, art directors, copy editors, and other staff members of *Fine Woodworking* who contributed to the development of the chapters in this book.

Contents

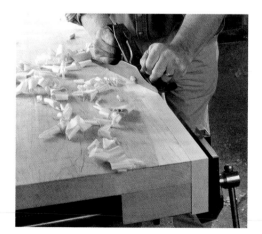

Introduction

Many woodworkers labor for years without a decent workbench, struggling to hold their workpieces in position and working at all kinds of uncomfortable angles. Even if they understand that a good bench is the center of an efficient and happy shop, they are probably just too busy making things to stop and make a serious woodworking bench.

If you have picked up this book, you've seen the light. And you've come to the right place.

Fine Woodworking has been outfitting woodworkers with smart and effective workbenches for 35 years, in styles to suit any mode of woodworking. Whether you are looking for a quick and easy workstation that will handle 90 percent of what you need, or a no-compromise traditional workbench that will look and function flawlessly for decades, there is a workbench here for you. And the magazine's wonderful exploded drawings and clear step-by-step photos will answer every question along the way, guaranteeing your success.

This collection of *Fine Woodworking*'s best workbenches doesn't stop there, however. After you wipe a coat of oil onto your gleaming new workbench, you'll open these pages again for a host of tips and jigs that will expand its capabilities even further.

—Asa Christiana
Editor, *Fine Woodworking*

The Workbench: An Illustrated Guide

GRAHAM BLACKBURN

In some parts of the world, woodworkers use the floor as their work surface. In Japan, it's a narrow beam. But in the West, woodworkers traditionally have used a substantial workbench. In fact, before tablesaws and routers became for most woodworkers their right and left hands, the workbench was the most important tool of the craft. Although it may no longer be the first tool a woodworker encounters in the shop, the workbench nevertheless remains at the heart of woodworking. A closer appreciation of its uses and strengths can do much to improve your woodworking experience, so here's a look at the development of the workbench, its major variations, and the many practical fixtures associated with its use.

The following are great moments in workbench history.

Roman bench

The prime purpose of the workbench is to facilitate the flattening and smoothing of stock, typically by planing. So it is no surprise that some of the earliest benches were used by the Romans 2,000 years ago, because it was the Romans who first made use of the metal-bodied plane. The Roman bench was little more than a long board supported by splayed legs and fitted with stops to prevent a board from being pushed off the bench during planing. This bench remained popular for more than four centuries after the demise of the Roman Empire and in some areas persists even today. The drawing is based on a photograph of a bench found in Saalburg, Germany, 250 B.C.

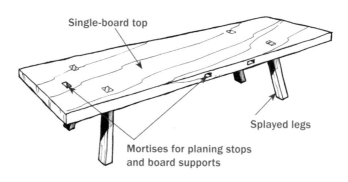

Single-board top

Mortises for planing stops
and board supports

Splayed legs

Sixteenth-century bench

After the Middle Ages, with the development of more sophisticated forms of furniture, benches grew larger and began to feature additional holding devices. By the 17th century, vises had become common in Northern Europe. German and Scandinavian benches, in particular, were fitted with vises very similar to the large wooden tail and face vises that were common on British benches until the introduction of metal vises. The drawing is based on one by Loffelholz, 1505.

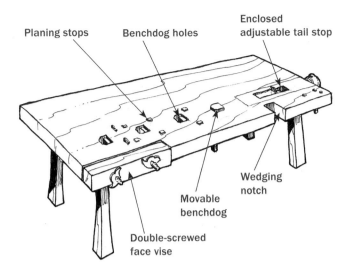

Planing stops   Benchdog holes   Enclosed adjustable tail stop

Wedging notch

Movable benchdog

Double-screwed face vise

Eighteenth-century French bench

One of the more distinctive varieties, the commonly used French bench was basically a heavy table that featured a tool rack, bench stops, side hooks, and holdfasts to secure the work; vises were a rarity.

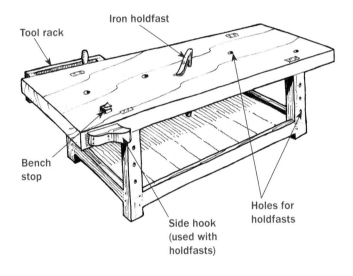

Tool rack   Iron holdfast

Bench stop

Side hook (used with holdfasts)

Holes for holdfasts

Eighteenth-century British bench

In contrast to French benches and most other European types, British benches from the 18th century relied heavily on a long face vise installed at the left end of the bench. This long vise frequently had a single screw and a guide rod to help keep it parallel, but sometimes it possessed two screws arranged so that the vise face could be angled for nonparallel stock. A stop and a holdfast also were common, but support for long boards held in the vise, in the form of apron pegs or a deadman, was distinctly British. This British-style bench immigrated to America with the early Colonists.

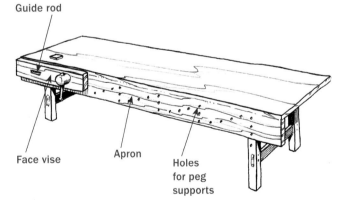

Guide rod

Face vise   Apron   Holes for peg supports

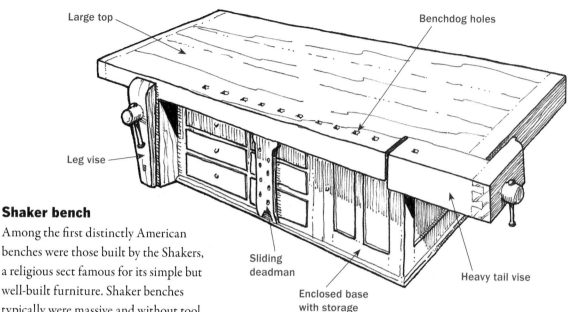

Large top

Benchdog holes

Leg vise

Sliding deadman

Enclosed base with storage

Heavy tail vise

Shaker bench

Among the first distinctly American benches were those built by the Shakers, a religious sect famous for its simple but well-built furniture. Shaker benches typically were massive and without tool trays, and because the Shakers valued order and neatness, their benches featured a base that was fully enclosed for storage. The Shakers also were fond of leg vises that could be kept parallel, unlike the garterless face vises previously common on workbenches. Because the cupboards and drawers in the base made the use of a bored apron impossible, the Shakers often used a sliding deadman to provide support for long workpieces.

Nineteenth-century school bench

The workbenches we use today owe much to the school bench that was common in the 19th and early 20th centuries. The essential features of this bench, whether single or double (like the one illustrated below), are a large work surface, usually with a trough or a tool well, both end and face vises (increasingly of the metal variety), and a system of benchdog holes in the top used for clamping workpieces.

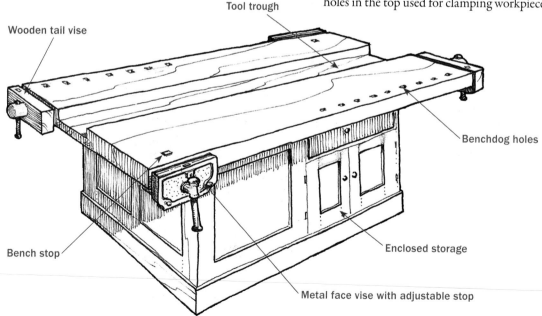

Tool trough

Wooden tail vise

Benchdog holes

Bench stop

Enclosed storage

Metal face vise with adjustable stop

Contemporary benches

Though there are countless variations, today's workbenches generally are based on either a cabinetmaker's bench or a Scandinavian-style bench.

Cabinetmaker's bench

Although many woodworkers prefer to build their own benches, the commercially made cabinetmaker's bench has become the standard. Consisting of a heavy-duty, laminated top, usually with a tool well, the cabinetmaker's bench is fitted with a benchdog system and a provision for holdfasts. Although the vises may have heavy wooden jaws, their screws are invariably metal, thus combining the best of both old and new.

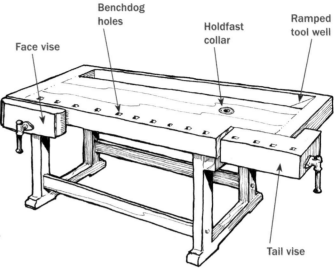

Face vise

Benchdog holes

Holdfast collar

Ramped tool well

Tail vise

Two rows of benchdog holes

Balanced twin-screw tail vise

Dogleg vise requires freestanding deadman support.

Scandinavian bench

A bench style popular with many woodworkers, the Scandinavian bench is fitted with either a standard tail vise or a balanced vise that can hold workpieces between benchdogs on both edges of the top, as shown. The Scandinavian bench is characterized by a dogleg face vise, considered by those who use it to be superior to the standard face vise because there are no screws to get in the way of the workpiece.

Vises

Most contemporary benches are fitted with vises. Although there are many varieties, certain things remain true for all vises. If the workpiece is to be held securely without being damaged, the jaws should be wooden or wood lined, clean, aligned, and parallel.

Tail vises

A tail vise holds a workpiece at the front of the bench. Newer tail vises that ride on a steel plate fixed to the bench can be adjusted so that the top and front of the vise remain flush with the top and front of the bench. Older tail vises ride on rails attached beneath the benchtop. Neither kind is designed to hold anything by the tail of the vise; doing so might misalign the vise. However, double-screwed end vises or end vises with a single screw and widely spaced guide arms can hold work against the end of the bench and, if they are as wide as the bench, can be fitted with benchdogs. A tail vise also can be used to clamp workpieces between a benchdog fixed in the benchtop and a dog fixed in the vise itself.

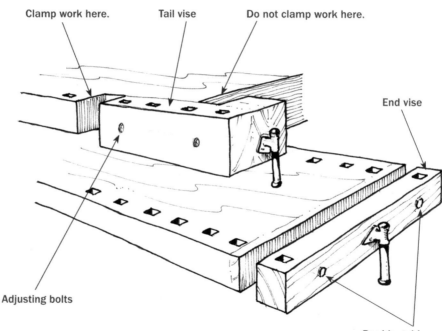

Clamp work here.   Tail vise   Do not clamp work here.

End vise

Adjusting bolts

Double guide arms

Face vises

A face vise is used for holding workpieces during planing. It works best if the inside faces of the jaws are flush with the front of the bench and if the tops of both jaws are flush with the surface of the bench. Although there will be occasions when you want to secure odd shapes (which can be done easily with purpose-made auxiliary jaws), the jaws should close perfectly parallel to each other so that they will hold even a thin sheet of paper firmly. Metal vises may need to be reset on the bench to meet these conditions, and they also may need to have their wood facings replaced. Wooden-jaw vises can be made flush more

easily. But before altering the jaws, examine the way your particular vise works and how it is attached to the bench.

Pay special attention to making sure the guide arms run smoothly with minimal play. Older wooden vises may need their guide arms resecured to the jaws and their guide blocks adjusted. Wooden screws depend on well-fitting garters and properly positioned threaded blocks. Providing they are properly aligned, newer vises with metal screws and guide arms have fewer problems and may need nothing more than occasional cleaning and lubrication.

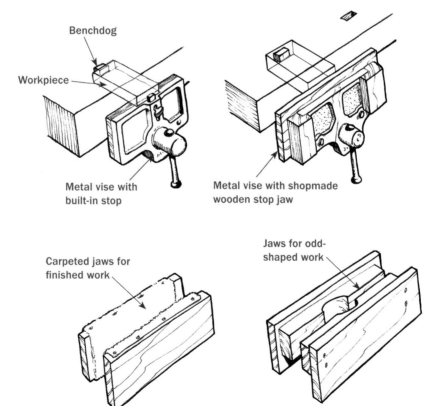

Some metal vises have built-in adjustable stops that can be used to clamp work between a benchdog and a stop in the benchtop. Vises that don't have adjustable stops can be fitted with a wooden stop jaw that will perform the same function or that can be custom-cut to hold other shapes.

Benchdog

Workpiece

Metal vise with built-in stop

Metal vise with shopmade wooden stop jaw

You may want to make various auxiliary jaws, such as carpeted jaws to hold finished work or jaws to hold round and odd-shaped pieces.

Carpeted jaws for finished work

Jaws for odd-shaped work

Bench accessories

A bench with vises, even when everything is in top condition and perfectly adjusted, is still only half the asset it might be—unless it's furnished with a variety of devices, such as benchdogs, holdfasts, and bench hooks.

Benchdogs

Metal dogs may last longer and fit better, but wooden dogs are easier to make and pose less of a threat to both tools and finished work surfaces. Side dogs also can be extremely useful for holding stock against the front apron.

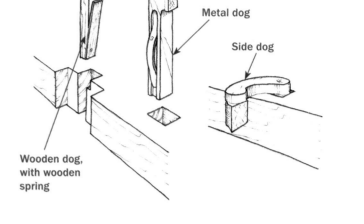

Metal dog

Side dog

Wooden dog, with wooden spring

Bench stops

A bench stop is designed to prevent the workpiece from being pushed off the bench. In its simplest form, it may be a small piece of scrap clamped or tacked anywhere on the bench. An integral stop, whether a simple wooden stop held in place and at the right height by friction, a wedge or simple screw, or one of the variously designed factory-made metal stops, is more convenient and often functions as the last stop in a line of benchdogs.

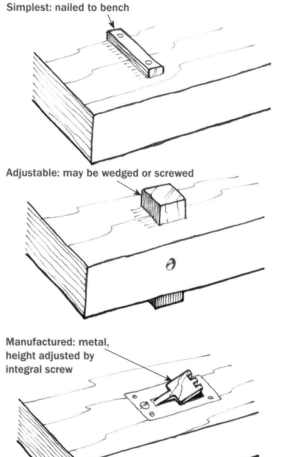

Simplest: nailed to bench

Adjustable: may be wedged or screwed

Manufactured: metal, height adjusted by integral screw

Holdfasts

A holdfast remains one of the most versatile pieces of equipment you can own. There are various modern forms available, but the simplest L-shaped iron bar inserted in any conveniently bored hole in the benchtop is efficient. Simply knock the top of the holdfast to secure the workpiece, and hit the back of the holdfast to release the workpiece. A holdfast's two main advantages are its ability to hold odd-shaped, flat, and rectangular pieces, and the fact that it can be positioned anywhere on the bench. Don't agonize over where to bore the first hole—you inevitably will need to bore another hole somewhere else. A particularly useful place is near a vise so that the vise and holdfast can be used together in a variety of ways. Older benches typically were bored in various places along the length.

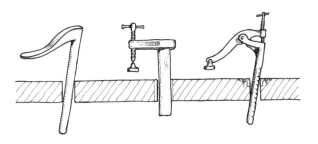

Simple angled iron in bored hole

Flat bar in sleeve

Fully adjustable in flush collar

Bench hooks

The most common device for securing small workpieces to the bench is the bench hook. This can be made in a variety of ways and may function as a simple sawing support, a sawing guide when kerfed exactly at 90 degrees, 45 degrees, or any other simple or compound angle, or as a convenient end-grain shooting block.

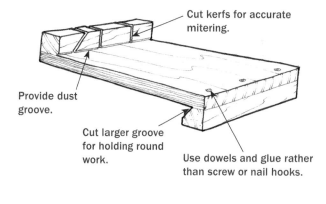

Cut kerfs for accurate mitering.

Provide dust groove.

Cut larger groove for holding round work.

Use dowels and glue rather than screw or nail hooks.

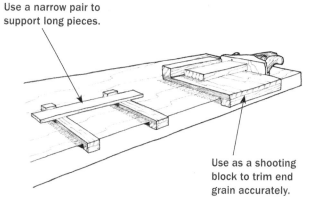

Use a narrow pair to support long pieces.

Use as a shooting block to trim end grain accurately.

Forget What You Know about Workbenches

JOSHUA FINN

When I opened my first shop 12 years ago after years of apprenticing with other woodworkers, one of my first decisions was about my bench. I needed something that could accommodate the usual handwork for furniture making—planing, chiseling, and sawing—but I also wanted a bench that could serve as a work station for machine setups and for glue-ups. This versatile bench was the solution.

The design is a combination of a couple of bench systems I had seen over the years. I worked in one cabinet shop in Brooklyn, N.Y., where the central assembly area was a set of fairly low benches with Homasote® 440 fiberboard tops. The soft Homasote protected the casework from dings, and the nonslip surface was ideal for sanding. I found the other piece of the puzzle in a friend's upstate New York shop: two torsion boxes held up by sawhorses, a space-saving idea that also offered flexibility and strength.

I took the important details from those shops, added a few ideas of my own, and incorporated them all into this bench system. It features two long, narrow torsion-box beams with Homasote tops and melamine bottoms that rest across two wide, sawhorse-type bases.

Although I have my father's classic bench, an old Hammacher Schlemmer® solid-maple workhorse with a face vise and a shoulder vise, it remains in my shop primarily for sentimental reasons. I now use this system for 98 percent of my benchwork. Even without vises and benchdogs, my bench design can accommodate any task that can be done on a traditional bench. It offers more flexibility, allowing me to set it up in different configurations for any job, and it can be broken down and stored out of the way. Plus the materials (2×4s, melamine, plywood, Homasote 440) are inexpensive (less than $150).

You can build this bench in less than a day, and you don't need a bench to make it (the usual conundrum when a beginner tries to make a big, traditional hardwood workbench).

Make the bases first

It makes sense to build the bases first, so you can assemble the beams on them. As you decide on a height for the bases, keep in mind the possibilities for multiple uses. Mine sometimes double as outfeed tables for my tablesaw. That height turns out to be a very comfortable working height for me. If your bases aren't going to do double duty as mine do, you should tailor their height to your own working preferences. In your calculations, don't forget to account for the extra 5 in. of the beams.

The bases are simple to build using glue and screws. The tops and stretchers are ¾-in.-thick plywood. The legs are made of 2×4s. But you can use solid furniture-grade lumber and mortise-and-tenon joinery if you wish.

Build the bases

The bases are easy to build using plywood and 2x4s. You can make them in a jiffy, then use them to assemble the torsion-box beams.

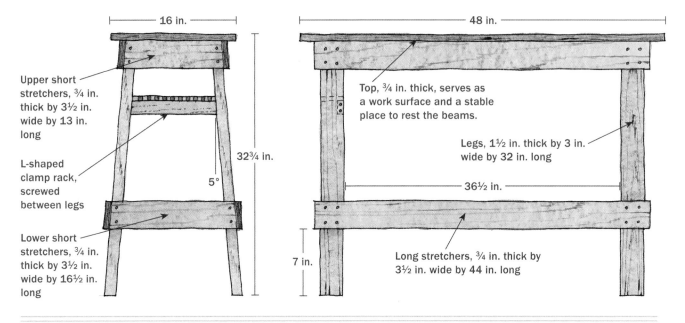

├─ 16 in. ─┤

Upper short stretchers, ¾ in. thick by 3½ in. wide by 13 in. long

L-shaped clamp rack, screwed between legs

Lower short stretchers, ¾ in. thick by 3½ in. wide by 16½ in. long

32¾ in.

5°

├──────── 48 in. ────────┤

Top, ¾ in. thick, serves as a work surface and a stable place to rest the beams.

Legs, 1½ in. thick by 3 in. wide by 32 in. long

├──── 36½ in. ────┤

7 in.

Long stretchers, ¾ in. thick by 3½ in. wide by 44 in. long

Angle the legs and side pieces. Cut a 5-degree bevel on the ends of the legs and a 5-degree angle on the ends of the short stretchers.

Two drills speed assembly. Start with the short stretchers and legs. Use the first to predrill with a countersink, the second to drive screws.

Glue and screw parts together. Sink only one of the four screws, then add the others once you square the long stretchers to the leg assembly.

Add the top and a clamp rack. The broad top supports the beams but also adds a handy work surface to the shop. The built-in rack keeps clamps close at hand.

Because this bench system relies on clamps for certain tasks, I added a simple L-shaped clamp rack to the side of each base. It's made from ⅜-in. Baltic-birch plywood with ⅜-in.-wide slots for the clamps. The sides of the rack are angled 5 degrees to fit between the legs of the base (see drawing on the facing page).

Begin construction by squaring up the 2×4 legs with light passes on the jointer and planer, just to take the framing lumber look from them. Next, use a miter saw to cut a 5-degree bevel on the tops and bottoms of the legs. The short stretchers also have the 5-degree angle cut on each end.

Start assembly by gluing and screwing the short stretchers flush to the outside of the legs. Then attach the long stretchers flush with the face of the side stretchers. Once the bases are assembled, screw on the tops, which add weight and stability. Finally, slide the clamp rack into position and secure it with screws.

Build the beams

After the bases are constructed, move on to the two beams that make up the top of the bench. The beams are plywood torsion

Beam construction

Two beams make for a flat, rigid work surface that switches from nonstick to non-marring by simply flipping the beams.

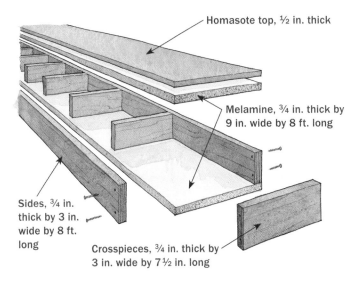

Homasote top, ½ in. thick

Melamine, ¾ in. thick by 9 in. wide by 8 ft. long

Sides, ¾ in. thick by 3 in. wide by 8 ft. long

Crosspieces, ¾ in. thick by 3 in. wide by 7½ in. long

Attach and smooth the melamine. Apply the melamine faces to both sides of the torsion box above, and soften the sharp edges with a file, left.

Assemble the nine crosspieces and two sides. Use clamps, moving them along the length as you work, to hold pieces flush and tight as you screw everything together.

Add the Homasote top. The inexpensive Homasote creates a non-marring work surface over the rigid ¾-in. melamine. The core of the melamine will grab screws when you need serious holding power.

boxes with ¾-in. melamine faces top and bottom, and Homasote over one of those faces. After cutting the parts to size, lay out the positions of the internal crosspieces, placing a crosspiece every 12 in. and at each end. Attach the crosspieces to one long side first, then the other. Keep all the edges flush (important when you attach the tops) by pinching them tight with a small bar clamp while predrilling and screwing. When the frame is finished, I screw melamine to the top and the bottom, and apply the Homasote on one side.

Made from recycled paper, Homasote is a cheap, easy-to-find material that's non-marring and grippy enough that an orbital sander can be used on a workpiece without router pads or stops. And when the surface gets worn from use, a quick sanding with 60-grit paper using the orbital sander refreshes it, or you can quickly remove it altogether and put on a fresh piece. The exposed melamine on the opposite side is an easy-to-clean surface for glue-ups.

Clamping versatility is unequalled. The beams can be moved apart to fit different widths. Access to all sides and the top and bottom of the work makes clamping easy. Flipping the beams melamine side up for gluing makes cleanup easy, too.

Using the bench

From hand-cutting dovetails to assembling kitchen-cabinet boxes, this bench is up to any task. It is totally portable and easily stored on end if you work in a small area and need the floor space. It can be easily reconfigured to accommodate any task. For example, the two beams can be pushed together to create an 8-ft. by 18-in. tabletop, or moved apart to any width when constructing cabinets. I can put the beams end-to-end to create a 16-ft.-long surface that is useful for shaping long handrails or other pieces of unusual length. Even without the beams resting on them, the 16-in.-wide by 48-in.-long tops on the bases can be used as a lower work surface, individually or together.

A 16-ft. bench. Arranging the bases and beams end-to-end gives long work, like this stair rail, a stable place to rest while it's being sanded.

Use a cleat. Screw scrapwood into the beams (top) to act as a stop and hold the system tight enough to handplane the surface of a board (see p. 12) or beltsand a newel post (above).

For most tasks, the weight of the beams and the bases (plus the wide tops of the bases) is enough to keep the system stable and in place. But for some jobs, such as handplaning the face or edge of a board, I clamp the workpiece to the beams and then clamp the beams to the bases. This locks everything in place so the forces I am applying don't move the workpiece or the bench.

To perform all the jobs possible that a traditional bench can handle, my bench system relies on clamps, screws, and cleats to hold the work in place. I hand-cut dovetails by clamping the pieces lengthwise to one of the beams. I handplane and scrape the faces of boards with the aid of a stop screwed into the beams. I use the same stop setup for beltsanding.

With this bench, it isn't necessary to devote permanent table space to benchtop

Lock it down for heavy planing. A clamp holds the beam and base together, stabilizing the whole system and preventing the beam from getting pushed off the base during handplaning. A second clamp holds the board (also resting across the bases for extra support) to the beam.

Handwork on smaller pieces. A hand screw clamped to the beam holds a smaller board on edge for planing (left). Drawer parts are clamped to the beam for sawing (above) or chopping.

machines and tools. I stow them until I need them and temporarily attach the tools to the beams when it's time to use them. I screw my dovetail jig down through the top for stability and to eliminate the need for clamps, which get in the way and tend to loosen with vibration. My mortiser gets attached the same way.

Clamping is easier than on a flat table or a traditional bench. You have the benefit of access all around and under the workpiece. There is no need for risers to get underneath the piece with clamps; the beams spread apart to accommodate different sizes (see the bottom photos on p. 16).

What's more, cleaning around and under the bench is simple because it's open and easily moved, and I haven't found a workbench out there that makes a better lunch table.

Sanding is a snap. Homasote is ideal as a sanding surface. It's soft enough that it won't mar workpieces, and it grips enough to hold your work without clamping it down, whether you are hand-sanding or using a random-orbit sander.

No clamps to get in the way. Screw benchtop machines and tools through the cheap Homasote and into the melamine below to temporarily hold them in place, eliminating the need for clamps that could get in the way or loosen with vibration.

Ready-Made Workbenches

MARK SCHOFIELD

At the heart of any woodworking shop is a solid workbench, but there has long been a debate over whether it's better to build your bench or buy it. Then there is the conundrum that you need a bench in order to build a bench. And if you think you can make a bench for a fraction of the cost of buying one, you may want to rerun the numbers: Remember that you can't buy 12/4 maple in bulk like a manufacturer can, and even if you handpick your boards, you'll have to cut away some knots, swirly grain, or checking. Add in the cost of some high-quality hardware and you'll find the savings melting away fast.

However, buying a workbench is rather like shopping for shoes: A single brand can have numerous models, the pros and cons of different features are not obvious without trying them out, and one size definitely doesn't fit all.

To help simplify the process of buying a bench, *Fine Woodworking* decided to test some models head-to-head. Because personal preference plays such a large role when selecting a workbench, rather than use a single author we decided to let all the editors have their say. Sure enough, opinions varied widely on some benches, but overall there was a consensus on the winners. If you are in the market for a workbench, this survey should help you pick one that suits you.

Editors get a feel for each bench. *Fine Woodworking*'s editors evaluated a bench's appearance and how well the vises worked. They also brought in their tools and gave each bench a good workout. As they planed, sawed, and chopped, they noted the sturdiness and rigidity of each bench, and how comfortable they found the working height.

How the benches were selected and tested

We chose benches approximately 6 ft. long by 2 ft. wide, with both a front and a tail vise, that were robust enough to stand up to the rigors of planing, chopping, and sawing by hand.

Six manufacturers or retailers supplied benches that met these criteria. Nearly all of them make or sell benches of different sizes and with other features than the ones we tested, so if you like the brand but not the bench, check their websites for alternatives. For the more subjective part of the test, the editors recorded how stable the bench felt, how well the vises worked, and how easy the dogs were to use. They also noted the general appearance of each bench; the quality of the finish; and the utility of any storage shelves, cabinets, or tool trays. When we were done, a straightedge, feeler gauges, combination square, and scales were used to objectively measure each bench.

Workbenches vary enormously. You really do have a wide choice when it comes to price, quality, and configuration. More than any other tool in your shop, a good workbench should last you a lifetime, so choose wisely.

One nice vise. The Lie-Nielsen tail vise's stiffness can be adjusted using a pair of bolts. The vise handles, with their black rubber O-rings to protect the turned cherry knobs from hitting the metal, earned unanimous praise.

Lie-Nielsen®: Custom made

Order one of these benches and you're unlikely to see its identical twin: Like a bespoke suit from Savile Row, each product is custom built to fit the owner's needs and desires. The owner can specify a top up to 8 ft. 4 in. long and 24 in. wide, with or without a tool tray, and any height. The tail vise can be positioned at either end, or you can specify a twin-screw tail vise at one or both ends with a double row of dog holes.

We ordered a traditional style of bench that was higher than most. Not surprisingly, a 6-ft. 3-in. member of our staff loved the height, but a surprising number of sub-6-ft. editors also found this height more relaxing to work at. Both vises earned high marks for their German hardware and their beautiful handles, which come complete with rubber O-rings to stop the turned cherry knobs from banging against the metal. The 50/50 boiled linseed oil and turpentine satin finish achieved the right balance of protecting the wood and being renewable.

This bench felt like it had been designed and built by a woodworker, and I think we'd all love to be able to boast that we'd made it ourselves. I suspect that this reason as well as the quality and the features made it our choice as best overall.

WWW.LIE-NIELSEN.COM
Length: 84 in.
Width: 24 in.
Height: 38 in.
Weight: 281 lb.
Wood: Maple
Editors' score: 8.5

WWW.HIGHLAND WOODWORKING.COM
Length: 71 in.
Width: 22 in.
Height: 34 in.
Weight: 162 lb.
Wood: European beech
Editors' score: 5.6

Hoffman & Hammer: 114102

The smallest, lightest, and cheapest of the benches we looked at, Hoffman & Hammer's medium bench could have been overshadowed by the heavyweight competition, but it stood its ground and earned the best-value award. The front vise in particular had very little racking. The main criticism was the lightness of the bench, particularly the base, which made the bench unstable when pushed from front to back (end-to-end planing pressure was no problem). A solution would be to install a tool cabinet in the base, although the elevated stretchers don't leave much room. The dogs and vises were small but worked smoothly, although the tail vise gradually increased in height as it was extended. This would be an ideal choice for someone looking for an economical, well-made workbench but without the physical mass.

Solid vise. The front vise displayed almost no racking when the workpiece was clamped at one end.

Dog versus drawer. When a dog is deployed in the central holes of the bench, it prevents the drawer from opening.

Grizzly®: H7725

WWW.GRIZZLY.COM
Length: 84 in.
Width: 24¾ in.
Height: 34¼ in.
Weight: 299.5 lb.
Wood: Birch
Editors' score: 4.4

This bench certainly looked different from all the rest. Instead of being made from large chunks of beech or maple, Grizzly's bench is made from thousands of strips of birch, most no larger than ¾ in. sq., laminated together. The top was relatively flat, and this method of construction should, in theory, make it the most stable of all the benches.

That's where the good news ends: Despite being the heaviest bench, when given a jolt it wobbled several times from end to end, probably due to the small stretchers and the undersize nuts and bolts that attach them to the legs. The front vise racked alarmingly, whereas the tail vise climbed ⅛ in. when tightened. When combined with the fact that the dogs leaned backward under pressure in their oversize holes, the effect was to raise the workpiece into the air.

The other trouble spot is the massive drawer in the base. Heavy even when empty, it is difficult to open when storing anything but bulky, light objects.

Laguna®: 7-ft. workbench

WWW.LAGUNA
TOOLS.COM
Length: 89½ in.
Width: 26½ in.
Height: 33 in.
Weight: 242.5 lb.
Wood: European beech
Editors' score: 6.5

The largest of the benches we tested, the Laguna also was the shortest. The overall appearance was pleasing and the bench had good stability, but on closer inspection the construction and the vises left something to be desired. The top was visibly wavy and dished 0.030 in. in several places, including the critical right-front corner near the tail vise, suggesting the top had been poorly wide-beltsanded. Also, the top of the trestle base protrudes beyond the front of the top, interfering when edge-planing a long board.

The dogs and dog holes got mixed reviews. Some editors described the fit as just right, whereas others found the dogs' flat spot too small to locate without a second glance. With some modest redesign and better quality control, this could become a much better bench.

Unsteady workpieces. A combination of slop in the tail vise and dogs that angle backward under pressure causes the workpiece to rise off the bench when clamped.

Good and bad dogs. The Laguna dogs slid in and out of the holes with the right amount of resistance, but editors disliked the small flat spot.

WWW.WOODCRAFT.COM
Length: 76½ in.
Width: 23⅝ in.
Height: 35½ in.
Weight: 279 lb.
Wood: European beech
Editors' score: 8.3

Sjoberg: Elite 2000

The Sjoberg only just missed the best-overall award. Initial comments were "handsome," "beautiful," "massive," and "well made," and closer inspection revealed a number of unique and useful features: The front vise can be switched to the opposite side of the bench and the bench rotated 180 degrees for left-handed use; square vise runners almost eliminated racking despite the nearly 2-ft. width of each vise; the legs are flush with the top and fitted with dog holes to allow wide boards to be supported when edge-planing. A heavy bench, the top is 3 in. thick with a 4-in.-thick apron, giving it a very sturdy feel. Uniquely, the front vise was also fitted with a pair of dog holes, which, combined with the holes running the length of the front and back sides, gives great clamping flexibility. The dogs were round with a large, flat clamping spot, but a little stiff and hard to remove when low in the hole. The only other complaint was the slightly rough and low-luster oil-finished surface, a minor blemish on an otherwise excellent bench.

Veritas®: 05A01.01

Opinions differed sharply on this bench, with nearly half the editors picking it as best value while others considered it overpriced. The most debated feature was the twin-screw tail vise—a Veritas exclusive. Proponents cited its lack of racking and ability to clamp a 15½-in.-wide board between the guides, and proclaimed it the best end vise on any bench. Skeptics called it weird, stiff, and jerky. The vise arrived unable to turn using one handle. Shop manager John White spent a few hours trying to tune it up and eventually reached a compromise between operating and not being too slack. The troubleshooting details in the manual suggest that our experience is not unique.

The center tool tray impressed some editors, but the design may be responsible for the bench being dished by 0.016 in. around the center. The dogs come with slip-on plastic tool protectors, but these prevented the dogs from being lowered less than an inch above the bench and must be removed when planing thinner stock. Finally, the shiny wipe-clean finish attracted some editors, but others wondered how it would look after a few years of use with no easy way to renew it. More than any other bench, this is probably one to try before you buy; you'll love it or leave it.

WWW.LEEVALLEY.COM
Length: 72¾ in.
Width: 26 in.
Height: 35 in.
Weight: 187 lb.
Wood: Maple
Editors' score: 6.8

Wide clamping ability.
The large distance between the guides in the tail vise allows wide boards to be clamped securely.

Edge-plane wide pieces.
The legs are flush with the sides of the benchtop and contain dog holes so they can support long boards.

A Workbench Thirty Years in the Making

GARRETT HACK

When I built my first bench well over 30 years ago, I had limited furniture-making experience, so I adapted the design from some benches I had used in various classes. That first bench has been a solid friend in the shop for many years. But as my experience level increased, I kept a mental list of improvements I'd make if I were to build a new one. I recently said as much in a lecture at Colonial Williamsburg, and *Fine Woodworking* decided to pay me to stop procrastinating.

Over the years, I've developed a love of hand tools. I use them in every aspect of furniture-making, and details made with these elegant tools are a signature of my work. So my first priority was to make the new bench better suited to my hand-tool habits.

What makes a bench work

In building this bench, I wanted a tool that would withstand the daily stresses heaped upon it, and the materials and design reflect that approach. A bench can be fashioned with humble materials (any dense and stable hardwood will do) and basic joinery and work very well.

Add beef

The benchtop is big enough to clamp a large case piece in almost any arrangement, with room for many tools, and it's thick and sturdy.

Peg the short rails. The trestles are assembled with beefy mortise-and-tenons. The rails are reinforced with hardwood pegs.

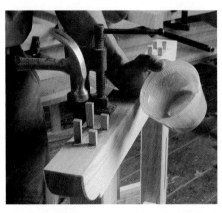

Wedge the shoes. The mortise-and-tenons in the top and bottom of the trestles are wedged.

Big stretchers. Threaded rod gives a secure connection between the stretchers and trestles.

Anatomy of a great bench

To build this bench, you'll need lots of clamps and glue. The trickiest parts will be the top (p. 30), which is built up in layers to get the 3-in. thickness, and the tail-vise assembly (p. 33). On the other hand, the trestle base is assembled with straightforward mortise-and-tenon joinery.

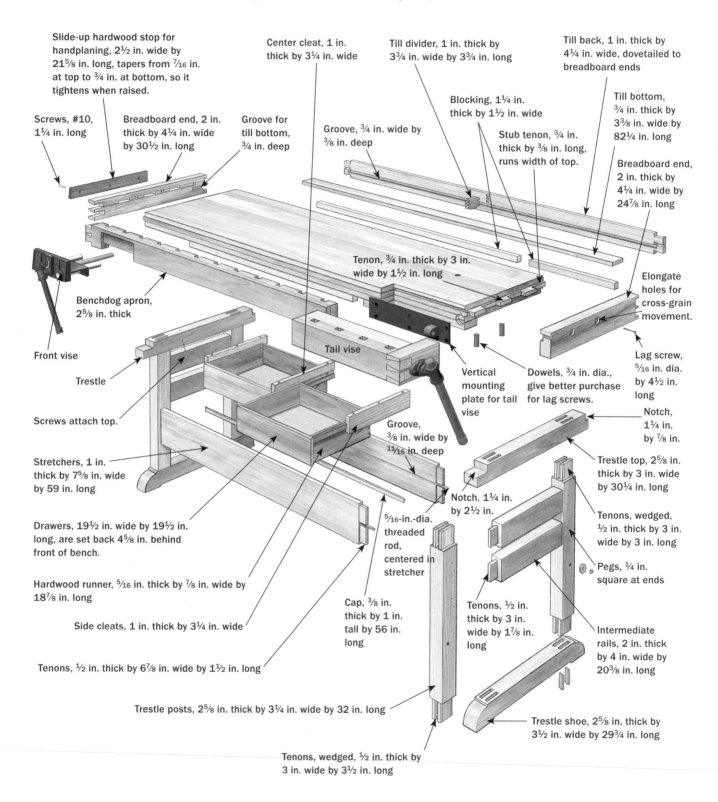

Slide-up hardwood stop for handplaning, $2\frac{1}{2}$ in. wide by $21\frac{5}{8}$ in. long, tapers from $\frac{7}{16}$ in. at top to $\frac{3}{4}$ in. at bottom, so it tightens when raised.

Screws, #10, $1\frac{1}{4}$ in. long

Breadboard end, 2 in. thick by $4\frac{1}{4}$ in. wide by $30\frac{1}{2}$ in. long

Groove for till bottom, $\frac{3}{4}$ in. deep

Center cleat, 1 in. thick by $3\frac{1}{4}$ in. wide

Groove, $\frac{3}{4}$ in. wide by $\frac{3}{8}$ in. deep

Till divider, 1 in. thick by $3\frac{3}{4}$ in. wide by $3\frac{3}{4}$ in. long

Blocking, $1\frac{1}{4}$ in. thick by $1\frac{1}{2}$ in. wide

Stub tenon, $\frac{3}{4}$ in. thick by $\frac{3}{8}$ in. long, runs width of top.

Till back, 1 in. thick by $4\frac{1}{4}$ in. wide, dovetailed to breadboard ends

Till bottom, $\frac{3}{4}$ in. thick by $3\frac{3}{8}$ in. wide by $82\frac{1}{4}$ in. long

Breadboard end, 2 in. thick by $4\frac{1}{4}$ in. wide by $24\frac{7}{8}$ in. long

Tenon, $\frac{3}{4}$ in. thick by 3 in. wide by $1\frac{1}{2}$ in. long

Benchdog apron, $2\frac{5}{8}$ in. thick

Front vise

Trestle

Screws attach top.

Tail vise

Vertical mounting plate for tail vise

Dowels, $\frac{3}{4}$ in. dia., give better purchase for lag screws.

Elongate holes for cross-grain movement.

Lag screw, $\frac{5}{16}$ in. dia. by $4\frac{1}{2}$ in. long

Notch, $1\frac{1}{4}$ in. by $\frac{7}{8}$ in.

Trestle top, $2\frac{5}{8}$ in. thick by 3 in. wide by $30\frac{1}{4}$ in. long

Stretchers, 1 in. thick by $7\frac{5}{8}$ in. wide by 59 in. long

Drawers, $19\frac{1}{2}$ in. wide by $19\frac{1}{2}$ in. long, are set back $4\frac{5}{8}$ in. behind front of bench.

Hardwood runner, $\frac{5}{16}$ in. thick by $\frac{7}{8}$ in. wide by $18\frac{7}{8}$ in. long

Side cleats, 1 in. thick by $3\frac{1}{4}$ in. wide

Tenons, $\frac{1}{2}$ in. thick by $6\frac{7}{8}$ in. wide by $1\frac{1}{2}$ in. long

Groove, $\frac{3}{8}$ in. wide by $\frac{11}{16}$ in. deep

Notch, $1\frac{1}{4}$ in. by $2\frac{1}{2}$ in.

$\frac{5}{16}$-in.-dia. threaded rod, centered in stretcher

Cap, $\frac{3}{8}$ in. thick by 1 in. tall by 56 in. long

Tenons, $\frac{1}{2}$ in. thick by 3 in. wide by $1\frac{7}{8}$ in. long

Tenons, wedged, $\frac{1}{2}$ in. thick by 3 in. wide by 3 in. long

Pegs, $\frac{1}{4}$ in. square at ends

Intermediate rails, 2 in. thick by 4 in. wide by $20\frac{3}{8}$ in. long

Trestle posts, $2\frac{5}{8}$ in. thick by $3\frac{1}{4}$ in. wide by 32 in. long

Tenons, wedged, $\frac{1}{2}$ in. thick by 3 in. wide by $3\frac{1}{2}$ in. long

Trestle shoe, $2\frac{5}{8}$ in. thick by $3\frac{1}{2}$ in. wide by $29\frac{3}{4}$ in. long

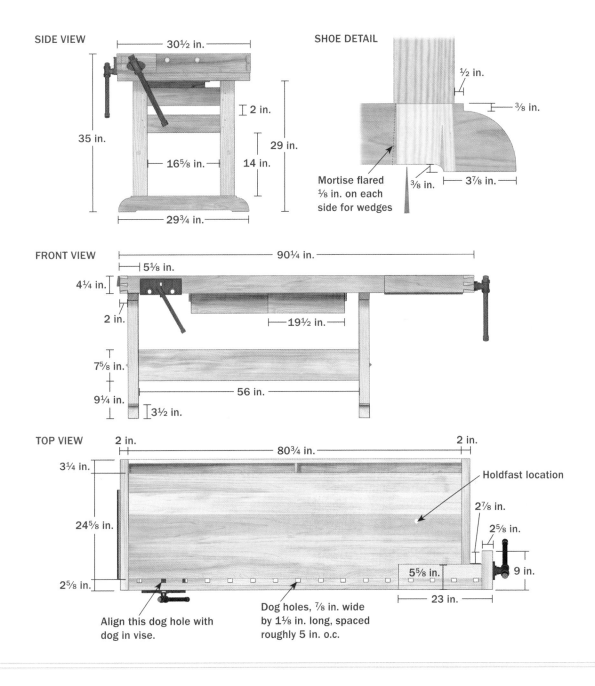

SIDE VIEW

30½ in.

2 in.

35 in.

29 in.

16⅝ in.

14 in.

29¾ in.

SHOE DETAIL

½ in.

⅜ in.

Mortise flared ⅛ in. on each side for wedges

⅜ in.

3⅞ in.

FRONT VIEW

90¼ in.

5⅛ in.

4¼ in.

2 in.

19½ in.

7⅝ in.

9¼ in.

56 in.

3½ in.

TOP VIEW

2 in.

2 in.

80¾ in.

3¼ in.

Holdfast location

2⅞ in.

24⅝ in.

2⅝ in.

5⅝ in.

9 in.

2⅝ in.

23 in.

Align this dog hole with dog in vise.

Dog holes, ⅞ in. wide by 1⅛ in. long, spaced roughly 5 in. o.c.

The base of the bench can hold a heavy load (the top weighs more than 200 lb.), but more important, it's rigid enough to withstand the racking forces created by handplaning.

At 35 in. tall, my bench will work for a wide range of tasks, from handwork to machine work to assembly jobs. But I'm over 6 ft. tall. You may have to experiment to find a comfortable height.

Lots of ways to hold work

Because I do a lot of handwork, I need surefire ways to hold workpieces. In my experience, the best tools for the job are a front vise and a tail vise, used in tandem with benchdogs and a holdfast. Finally, I added a sliding stop at the left end. It can be set high or low and is useful for planing panels, thin drawer bottoms, tabletops, or multiple parts.

Section through top

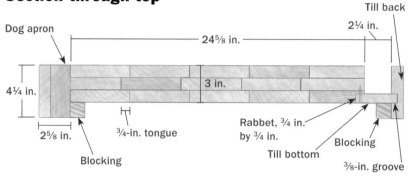

Dog apron

24⅝ in.

Till back

2¼ in.

4¼ in.

3 in.

2⅝ in.

¾-in. tongue

Blocking

Rabbet, ¾ in. by ¾ in.

Till bottom

Blocking

⅜-in. groove

First section kicks it off. Glue the first three boards together, then let the assembly dry. Clean up squeeze-out so it won't interfere with the following section.

Three boards at a time. After the glue dries from each previous section, add the next three boards, applying glue to all mating surfaces. Clamp across the faces and edges. Repeat until the whole slab of the top is assembled. You'll need lots of clamps. Use cauls to keep the assembly flat.

Build the top on a pair of strong horses

The top looks like a bunch of 12/4 planks glued together, but it's actually three layers of 1-in.-thick boards. This design is very stable so it will stay flat, and it's an economical way to use materials. I used hard maple, yellow birch, and beech, dedicating the best of the maple to the top layer and the breadboard ends, and using narrower and somewhat lower-quality material for the middle and bottom layers.

Glue up the top one section at a time. To make the job less stressful, I recommend Unibond® 800, a slow-setting urea-formaldehyde glue (www.vacupress.com) typically used in vacuum veneering. Once you have the top glued together, use a circular saw to trim the benchtop to length. Clean up the edges with a scraper and a handplane, and flatten the top. When the top is flat, rout the rabbet for the till bottom on the back lower edge.

How to handle big breadboards. After mortising the breadboard pieces, cut the tongue and tenons on the top. Use a router and fence to make the cheek cuts (left) and a handsaw to remove the waste between the long tenons. Clean out the corners with chisels (right).

Make the benchdog apron

The benchdog apron is laminated from two pieces. After gluing the pieces together, lay out and cut the mortise for the front vise hardware in the apron; depending on the vise, you may need to cut a hollow under the top to accommodate the hardware. Once that's done, use a dado set to cut the dog holes. Attach the vise's rear jaw to the apron and then set the piece aside as you start working on the breadboard ends.

Breadboard ends are next

Cut the breadboard ends to width and thickness but leave them a bit long. Cut them to size after you lay out and cut the joinery to attach them to the benchtop. At the rear of each breadboard, rout the groove for the till bottom; it should align with the rabbet in the benchtop. Then drill holes for the lag screws that will help anchor the breadboards to the top. Finally, lay out and cut the dovetails.

Use a router and fence to cut the tenon cheeks on the ends of the top. Then lay out and cut the long tenons that will go deep into the breadboards. Clean up the inside corners with a chisel, and fine-tune the fit using handplanes.

Once the breadboards have been fitted, drill the pilot holes for the lag screws. To give the screws extra purchase (so they don't just go into weak end grain), I mortised hardwood dowels from under the benchtop, in line with the pilot holes.

Attach the breadboards, apron, and till

Start by gluing the apron to its breadboard end. Then apply glue to the apron and front edge of the benchtop. Screw on the breadboard end and clamp the apron in place, working from the corner out. Don't worry about exactly where the apron ends; you'll be notching out that end of the benchtop for the tail vise. Finally, install the other breadboard end.

Start at the front left corner. Connect the breadboard to the apron (above left). Then apply glue to the breadboard tenons and to the interior face of the apron. Go lightly to avoid squeeze-out into the dog holes. Clamp the breadboard in place to help support the long dog apron (top right), then drive in the lags. The right-hand corner of the top (reversed at bottom right) will be notched for the tail vise, so there's no need to make the dog apron the full length of the bench.

After the glue cures on the breadboard ends and the benchdog apron, install the till parts and 1× blocking underneath, which increases stiffness and gives better clamp purchase.

Assemble the base

Once the top has been glued together, build the trestles and make the stretchers for the base. Before gluing and wedging the top of the trestles, notch both ends to go around the benchdog apron in front and the till in back.

Add the tail vise

Building a smooth-working tail vise can take nearly as long as building the benchtop or base. The work is worthwhile because a tail vise is unmatched at holding work flat on the benchtop between dogs. Have the hardware in hand before you start and make a full-scale drawing of the whole assembly to make layout easier. Use a circular saw and hand tools to cut a notch in the benchtop for the vise, and tune the vertical surfaces square with the top. Rout the groove for the top plate (see the top photo below) a bit oversize to provide a little clearance and leave room for adjustment, if needed. Now attach the vertical mounting plate to the bench (with only two screws so you can adjust it later if need be), aligned with the top-plate slot and perfectly parallel with the benchtop.

The till goes on last. Screw the till bottom into its rabbet under the top. Glue the divider in the till back, then glue the assembly to the breadboard ends and the top.

Make way for the top plate. Use a three-wing slot cutter to rout a groove parallel to the benchtop to house the top plate. The vertical board tacked in the corner acts as a spacer to prevent the bit from cutting too far.

Attach the vertical plate. Clamp the bottom plate in place. Align the top of the vertical plate with the groove, drill pilot holes, and drive in the top screws. Now attach the top and bottom plates and try the sliding action.

Core of the Vise

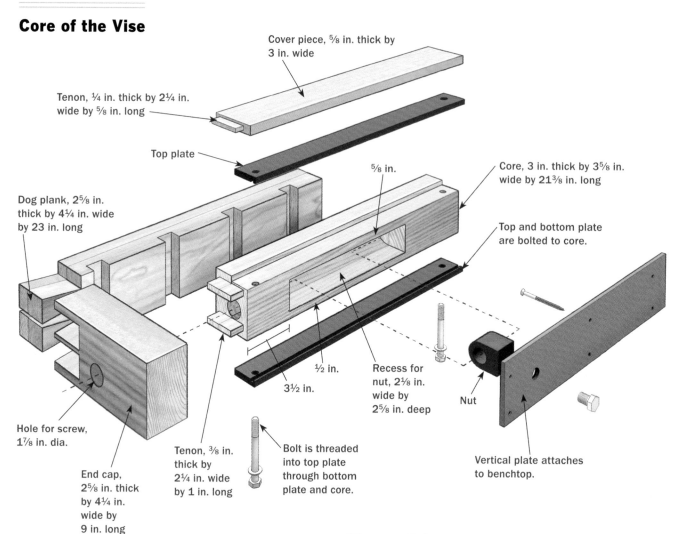

Cover piece, ⅝ in. thick by 3 in. wide

Tenon, ¼ in. thick by 2¼ in. wide by ⅝ in. long

Top plate

Dog plank, 2⅝ in. thick by 4¼ in. wide by 23 in. long

⅝ in.

Core, 3 in. thick by 3⅝ in. wide by 21⅜ in. long

Top and bottom plate are bolted to core.

Hole for screw, 1⅞ in. dia.

End cap, 2⅝ in. thick by 4¼ in. wide by 9 in. long

Tenon, ⅜ in. thick by 2¼ in. wide by 1 in. long

Bolt is threaded into top plate through bottom plate and core.

½ in.

3½ in.

Recess for nut, 2⅛ in. wide by 2⅝ in. deep

Nut

Vertical plate attaches to benchtop.

CROSS-SECTION

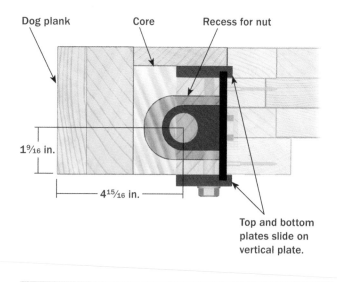

Dog plank

Core

Recess for nut

1⁹⁄₁₆ in.

4¹⁵⁄₁₆ in.

Top and bottom plates slide on vertical plate.

The core is key

The core of the vise accommodates the screw and nut, and is laminated from two pieces. Before gluing them together, hollow out the interior of one piece with a core-box bit and router. The other piece has a rectangular section removed with a saw. Glue these two pieces together and let them dry.

Now make the dog-hole plank and dovetail it to the end cap. Cut two mortises in the end cap and mating tenons on the end of the core, for alignment and added strength. Also, cut the shallow mortise into the end cap and a tenon on the end of the top cover. Cut a shallow rabbet in the top edge for the top guide plate.

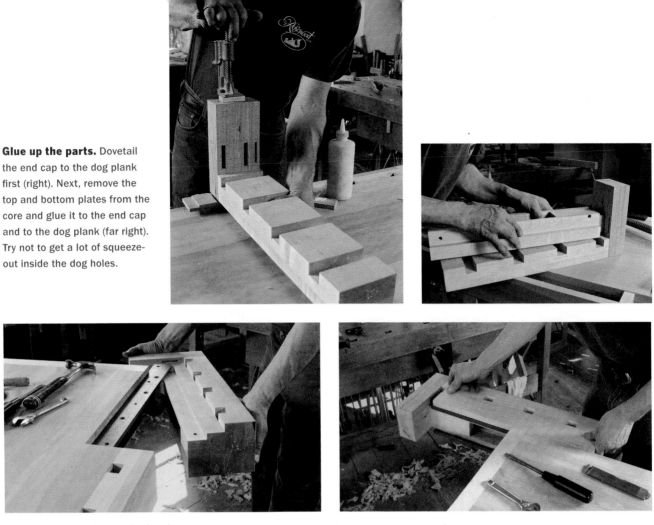

Glue up the parts. Dovetail the end cap to the dog plank first (right). Next, remove the top and bottom plates from the core and glue it to the end cap and to the dog plank (far right). Try not to get a lot of squeeze-out inside the dog holes.

Mount the wood jaw to the hardware. Be sure to clean up the wood parts to remove any glue squeeze-out that could interfere with the assembly (above left). Thread the bolts through the core, and then screw each plate to the core. Glue the top cover to the core and to the end cap (above right).

Attach the top and bottom guide plates to the core and slide it onto the plate on the bench. Test the action—there should be little wiggle when you lift the front edge, and the core should move parallel to the bench. If the guide plates grip the steel plate on the bench too tightly, the core movement will be stiff. Shim the bottom guide plate with a piece of veneer or a business card. If you have lots of wiggle, the plates need to be tighter together, so deepen the rabbet for the top guide into the core slightly and retest.

Add the dog plank and top

When the core moves smoothly, remove it from the bench. Now glue the dog-hole plank and end cap together and to the core. Mount the assembly to the benchtop, adding the last screws to the mounting plate. Thread in the lead screw and fasten the flange to the end cap and test the vise action. Finally, install the top piece, which is tenoned into the end cap and glued to the top of the core.

Final details

Now finish the surface prep on the benchtop. Bring all surfaces flush and smooth using handplanes. I chamfered all edges with a block plane. Add the slide-up stop on the end of the bench, install the drawers, and make a couple of handles for your vises. Last, finish the top with two coats of boiled linseed oil.

The Essential Workbench

LON SCHLEINING

Several *Fine Woodworking* editors and I collaborated on designing an essential workbench for today's woodworker, one that is straightforward to build without compromising performance. This bench was designed to be a tool—more workhorse than showpiece. We did not include traditional components simply for history's sake, and we took advantage of modern innovations. We also wanted this bench to be a project that most woodworkers could build using tools found in an average small shop: tablesaw, portable planer, crosscut saw, router, drill press, and hand tools. The only heavy-duty tool I used was a 3-hp tablesaw. Ripping lots of 8/4 maple puts a strain on even a large saw, so use a clean, sharp blade.

Components of the essential workbench

Avid woodworkers themselves, the *Fine Woodworking* editors regularly visit shops across the country, and they see a wide array of workbench configurations. Like all woodworkers, they know what they like and don't like. In the end we all compromised a bit, but we reached a solid consensus—a durable workbench requires beefy parts.

A thick, solid top

We decided on an overall size of 28 in. wide by 6 ft. long. Add a few inches for vise jaws, and it's a nice, big top. The editors thought

Anatomy of a workbench

This bench consists of the following (and construction proceeds in this order): a trestle base joined with mortise-and-tenons; a thick top laminated from boards set on edge; and front and end vises, both with wood jaws.

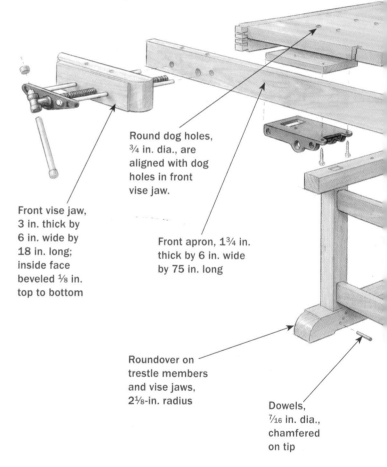

Round dog holes, ³⁄₄ in. dia., are aligned with dog holes in front vise jaw.

Front vise jaw, 3 in. thick by 6 in. wide by 18 in. long; inside face beveled ¹⁄₈ in. top to bottom

Front apron, 1³⁄₄ in. thick by 6 in. wide by 75 in. long

Roundover on trestle members and vise jaws, 2¹⁄₈-in. radius

Dowels, ⁷⁄₁₆ in. dia., chamfered on tip

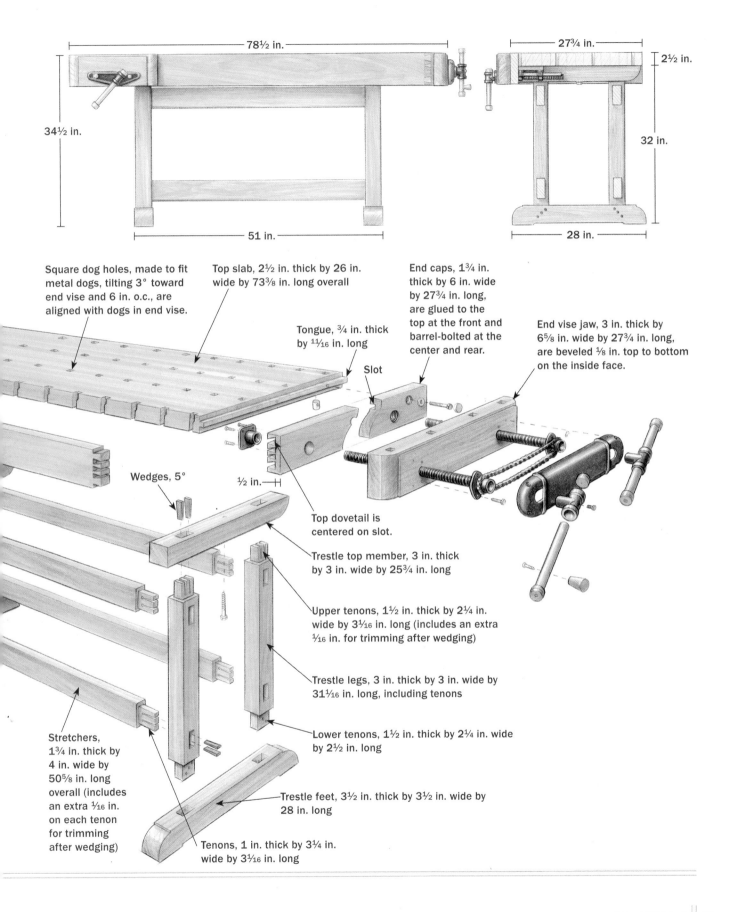

78½ in.

34½ in.

51 in.

27¾ in.

2½ in.

32 in.

28 in.

Square dog holes, made to fit metal dogs, tilting 3° toward end vise and 6 in. o.c., are aligned with dogs in end vise.

Top slab, 2½ in. thick by 26 in. wide by 73⅜ in. long overall

End caps, 1¾ in. thick by 6 in. wide by 27¾ in. long, are glued to the top at the front and barrel-bolted at the center and rear.

End vise jaw, 3 in. thick by 6⅝ in. wide by 27¾ in. long, are beveled ⅛ in. top to bottom on the inside face.

Tongue, ¾ in. thick by 11/16 in. long

Slot

Wedges, 5°

½ in.

Top dovetail is centered on slot.

Trestle top member, 3 in. thick by 3 in. wide by 25¾ in. long

Upper tenons, 1½ in. thick by 2¼ in. wide by 3 1/16 in. long (includes an extra 1/16 in. for trimming after wedging)

Trestle legs, 3 in. thick by 3 in. wide by 31 1/16 in. long, including tenons

Lower tenons, 1½ in. thick by 2¼ in. wide by 2½ in. long

Stretchers, 1¾ in. thick by 4 in. wide by 50⅝ in. long overall (includes an extra 1/16 in. on each tenon for trimming after wedging)

Trestle feet, 3½ in. thick by 3½ in. wide by 28 in. long

Tenons, 1 in. thick by 3¼ in. wide by 3 1/16 in. long

2 in. in top thickness would be plenty, with extra thickness at the edges, but I made this top 2½ in. thick because it wasn't much more difficult to mill and laminate thicker pieces. However, if you start with a premade bench slab, the standard 1¾-in. thickness offers plenty of mass and solidity for serious hand-tool use, especially after adding the thicker apron and end caps.

Gluing up the slab allowed me to machine the square dog holes before the pieces were assembled. Round dog holes might be a better option for a premade slab because square ones are best cut while the top slab is in pieces.

A heavy, rigid base

I wanted the benchtop and base to be nicely proportioned. Many benches I've seen look like top-heavy slabs on spindly legs. Also, it was important that the bench not rack or skid across the floor under heavy hand-planing. A thick trestle base, joined with pinned or wedged mortise-and-tenons, guarantees stability. I laminated 8/4 lumber to make these thick members (and the top slab) because 8/4 is readily available in most regions.

Splitting the stretchers, two high and two low, leaves a perfect opening for a future cabinet with drawers. The traditional single, wide stretcher would have saved some time, but it also would have blocked this natural storage area.

Innovative vises

Hundreds of woodworkers probably would say they could not get through a day without a conventional tail vise, which is designed primarily for clamping things flat on the benchtop between dogs. Others would say the same for a shoulder vise, which offers the capability of clamping workpieces between its jaws without interference from guide bars or screws. The Veritas Twin-Screw Vise incorporates some of the capabilities of both types, allowing long boards or large panels to be clamped with benchdogs as well as clamping an upright board up to 15 in. wide for operations such as dovetailing. The two screws are connected with a chain, preventing the jaws from racking no matter where a workpiece is located or which row of dog holes is used.

I've always loved the look and performance of thick wooden jaws on a front vise but found it tedious to crank the long screw in and out constantly. I was tempted to install a cast-iron, quick-action Record-style vise, until I found a German-made quick-action vise screw and guide bars at Woodcraft®. That allowed me to design a wooden front jaw to match the one I made for the Veritas end vise and still have quick action. However, a cast-iron vise also would have been fine (see pp. 118–123 for proper installation), and a patternmaker's vise is an interesting option.

Both square and round benchdogs

The debates over round versus square and wood versus metal will go on as long as folks work wood. All dogs have advantages, but I prefer square, steel ones. However, lots of accessories are designed to fit into ¾-in. round holes, so I incorporated both types into the bench. For the end vise, I milled square dog holes to fit specific steel dogs. But I can make wood ones if I choose, fitting them to the holes for the metal dogs. I ran two rows of ¾-in. round dog holes for the front vise. This gives me the option of using round dogs as well as hold-downs and holdfasts, which use ¾-in. holes. The round dog holes also provide the option of locating and securing jigs with ¾-in. dowel pins.

A tool tray is optional

I like tool trays, but many woodworkers think they are only good for collecting debris. Although this design lacks one, a tool tray could be attached easily to the back of the benchtop. Keep in mind that the large space between the stretchers will house a small chest of drawers for protected storage close at hand.

Build the base first

It's more glamorous to build the top than the base. But if you build the base first, you can use it for gluing up the top slab. Then, when the top is ready, you can set it on the base to finish installing the vises. Wedged mortise-and-tenons join the legs and stretchers, creating strong resistance to racking; pegged mortise-and-tenons join legs to feet. Laminating two layers of 8/4 material (each 1¾ in. thick after surfacing) creates the right thickness for the base members. Mill the legs and top crossmembers down to 3 in. square, but leave the feet at 3½ in. square.

Base assembly. The feet are pinned to the legs. Start by drilling the dowel holes in the feet, dry-fitting the joints, and transferring (above) the dowel-hole locations to the tenons. Then use a center punch (below left) to offset those locations slightly on the tenons, creating the draw effect. Last, apply glue to all surfaces, assemble the joint, and drive home the dowels (below right).

A jig makes easy work of mortises

There are 16 mortises (and tenons) in the base but only two different sizes. Make two mortising jigs to speed up layout and guide the chisels. The jig is made from three blocks glued and screwed together, with a fence attached on each side to hug the workpiece.

Locate and lay out the mortises. With the jig, this job should go quickly.

Drill out most of the waste. The layout lines will guide you. For the blind mortises, set the drill press's depth stop.

Chop out the rest with chisels. Remove most of the material with a ½-in. chisel before switching to a wider one. The jig will guide the chisels precisely.

Leave the stretchers the full 1¾ in. in thickness and rip them ⅜ in. oversize in width to allow them to move. When a wide plank is ripped into narrower pieces, tension in it is released, resulting in boards that bow one way or the other. Let the stretcher stock sit for two days, straighten and rip it to rough width, then run it through a portable planer on edge to clean each edge and bring the pieces to final width. If there's any fitting to be done, it's easier to do it on the tenons, so cut the mortises first, using a four-sided guide block to help with the chisel work (see "A jig makes easy work of mortises" above).

Then cut the tenons on the tablesaw, using a dado set.

Cutting the thumbnail profile

For the next task, cutting a large thumbnail profile on the feet, it will be worth your time to install a sharp new blade on the bandsaw. Before cutting the curve, I used a tablesaw and a crosscut sled to cut the small step at the top of the profile. After the bandsaw cut, the smoothing went quickly using a rasp and some files, followed by sandpaper.

Assembling the base

Start with the two trestle assemblies; it's critical that they be flat and square. After the dowels have been driven home and the glue has set, dry-fit and then glue and wedge the stretchers in place. Put glue in the mortises and on the tenons as well as on the wedges and in the wedge slots. At every step of the way, measure diagonally to make sure everything stays square, and sight across the trestle tops to be sure the assembly doesn't twist as you clamp it. Your eye will pick up minute variations.

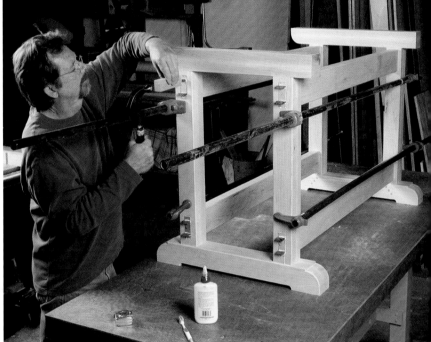

Through-tenons are wedged. Wedge the top members and stretchers. The slots in the tenons are angled 5 degrees to match the wedge angle. A hole is drilled at the base of each slot to prevent splitting. Apply glue to all surfaces, including the wedges and slots; assemble the joint; and drive home the wedges (above), using a block of wood to protect them from direct blows. Last, connect the two trestles with the upper and lower stretchers (right), wedging their tenons in place.

Make up the top slab in sections. First, joint and plane the pieces. Run them through the planer on edge to ensure uniformity (left). Then, glue up three sections of five boards. The base makes a level glue-up platform, but protect it from drips. Use a notched card to spread glue (center). Use cauls to keep the slab flat. Wrap them with clear tape for easy cleanup. Snug them down first, then clamp across the width (right).

Milling benchdog holes

Cut the holes for the square benchdogs with a dado blade before glue-up. The notches for the dog faces can be routed or chopped out with a chisel.

Dado the dog holes. Use a crosscut sled with a wedge against the fence to cut the slots at a 3-degree angle. A square pin sets the distance between dog slots.

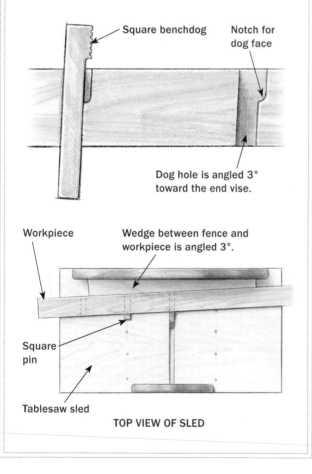

Square benchdog

Notch for dog face

Dog hole is angled 3° toward the end vise.

Workpiece

Wedge between fence and workpiece is angled 3°.

Square pin

Tablesaw sled

TOP VIEW OF SLED

Build the top in sections

The boards for the top are plainsawn 8/4 stock set on edge and laminated face to face. The top's finished thickness is 2½ in., but you should expect some bowing when you rip the boards from wider stock, so rip the boards for the slab just under 3 in. wide. Once the strips have stabilized for a day or two, joint them straight on one edge, rip them on the tablesaw to about 2¾ in., and then plane them on edge to about 2⅝ in. This leaves the pieces ⅛ in. oversize to allow for finish planing after each section is glued up. Cut the slots for the square dogs now, while the pieces are separate.

Most woodworkers have a portable surface planer capable of planing a 12-in.-wide board. So glue up and mill the 26-in. top slab in three sections of five boards, each able to fit through the planer and easier to handle than the full slab.

Clamping with cauls is a two-step process. First, align the boards by applying clamp pressure to the cauls. After the boards are in line, clamp them together horizontally. Aside from straight cauls, the other key to success is a flat gluing surface. The top cross-members on the base form the perfect platform to prevent the top from twisting during glue-up.

A damp (not wet) toothbrush makes short work of cleaning the glue out of the dog holes as long as this is done immediately after the slab is clamped up. Once the glue has set for an hour or so, remove the cauls and scrape off the excess glue. Let each slab cure overnight before moving on to the next one.

Plane the sections before gluing up the entire slab

If the cauls have been placed correctly, the glued slab sections should be flat with no twist. Remove any leftover glue from the top surfaces. Then, with the top surface of

Flatten the slab. A five-board section of the top slab is narrow enough to fit through a benchtop planer.

Now glue three sections into one big slab. Place a try square across the dog holes and use a long bar clamp diagonally to correct any misalignment. Again, use lots of clamps and cauls to keep the sections level.

Trim the ends of the top in two steps. Use the simple two-fence jig shown. Rout deep slots in both sides of the slab (top), then use a jigsaw to cut off the waste (bottom), leaving square shoulders and a tongue that will fit into the end caps.

the slabs down on the planer bed, run them through, taking light cuts until the bottom surface is clean. Turn the slabs top-surface-up and run them through again, taking light cuts until the top surface is clean. Turn them over once more and plane the underside until you reach the 2½-in. thickness.

Gluing together the slabs is a lot like gluing up the individual sections. Again, use the top crossmembers on the base and lots of cauls to keep the pieces aligned. Then it's simple to close the last of the glue joints. However, check the dog-hole locations with a square to be sure they all will be the same distance from the end vise.

A trick for trimming the slab to length

Not many of us own a saw capable of accurately crosscutting a very heavy slab almost 2½ ft. wide and more than 6 ft. long. For this project, a simple router jig will allow you, in one operation, both to trim each end accurately and to create some necessary joinery (see the right-hand photos above). By cutting deep dadoes on the top and bottom of the slab, a tongue is formed, which fits into a slot milled into the end cap. Cut the remaining ¾-in. tongue to length with a jigsaw (not an important glue surface so not a critical cut). Cut the mating slots in the end caps using a dado set on the tablesaw.

Install the end caps and front apron

The end caps cover the end grain of the top slab and help keep the slab flat. The right-hand end cap also serves as the rear jaw for the end vise. The front apron beefs up the thickness at this critical work area and serves as the rear jaw for the front vise. I not only needed a strong mechanical joint holding the front apron to the end caps, but I also wanted the areas that act as vise jaws to remain flat, with no end grain protruding, as it would if I used through-dovetails or finger joints at the corners. Half-blind dovetails seemed to be the perfect solution, oriented as shown in the drawing on pp. 36–37.

After cutting the joinery but before gluing the end caps and front rail in place, use a drill press to bore the holes for the vise hardware. Mount the end caps with cross-barrel bolts. The Veritas vise includes four of these; use two for each end cap. Apply glue only along the front 3 in. or 4 in. of the tongue and the groove. This limits wood movement of the slab toward the back of the bench.

The front apron is attached to the slab with glue only (and help from the half-blind dovetails).

Mount the vises and attach the top

Both vises come with thorough instructions, making the hardware straightforward to mount. The twin-screw vise attaches to the bench rather simply, with its two large screws passing through large nuts attached to the inner face of the end cap. It's critical that holes in the front and rear jaws align perfectly, so drill them at the same time. The length of the chain determines the distance between holes, so careful layout is in order. The vertical location of the holes is determined by adding 1½ in. to the thickness of the top slab to allow the large vise nuts to clear the underside of the benchtop.

Cut the right-hand set of half-blind dovetails. First, cut the tails in the front apron, and then clamp the front apron in place with the right-hand end cap behind it to transfer the layout of the dovetails.

Attach the large vise nuts to the back of the end cap. Also, finish cutting and fitting the dovetails.

Now for the front vise. Start by attaching the mounting bracket under the benchtop. The blocking under the bracket will increase the clamping capacity.

Locate the clearance holes in the front apron. Clamp the front apron accurately in place and tap a brad-point drill bit through the holes in the hardware to transfer their locations. Drill the holes in the front apron and front vise jaw at the same time.

Attach the front-vise hardware to the front jaw. Use the vise hardware to clamp the front jaw in its proper position before drilling for the attachment screws. Last, cut the half-blind dovetails on the left-hand end cap and attach the end cap.

Mounting the front-vise hardware and the large wood jaw is even more straightforward. First, the mounting bracket must be bolted to the underside of the benchtop. I used 5/16-in. lag screws. Next, the vise screw and guide bars are run through the bracket to locate their clearance holes in the front rail. Last, make the large wood jaw and bolt it to the vise hardware. Somewhere along the way, the front jaws for both vises must receive their large thumbnail profile, identical to the one on the trestle feet.

Once you have all of the hardware and vises in place, mill a 1/8-in. bevel on each of the outside jaws to accommodate flex in the hardware as the jaws tighten, which helps them maintain good clamping pressure at the top. Now you can attach the top to the base. Two lag bolts along the centerline of the bench are plenty for attaching the benchtop to the trestle base.

Flatten the top and finish the bench

Do the final flattening after the top has been mounted to the base and all of the vises are in place. If your glue-ups went well, all you will

Assemble the hardware for the twin-screw end vise. Clips join the chain at the proper length. Again, use the vise hardware to clamp the jaw in position before drilling for the attachment screws.

have to do is some scraping and sanding.

I didn't want a slick finish, as beautiful as it might be. Clamps, hold-downs, and vises depend on friction to hold parts securely. The traditional finish for a benchtop is linseed oil thinned with turpentine, which seals the wood enough to make glue removal pretty easy but doesn't make the surface more slippery than it is naturally. However, I wiped on a thinned varnish for greater protection. To make sure moisture absorption is even on all sides, it's important to coat the top and underside of the bench equally.

Tool Cabinet for a Workbench

LON SCHLEINING

It's exasperating when I can't find a tool. Usually I know it's in a pile somewhere, or on a shelf, or over there where I think I saw it last. Well, all that frustration is behind me now. After 27 years as a professional woodworker, I finally have a real tool chest.

When "The Essential Workbench" (pp. 36–45) was designed, the stretchers were deliberately positioned to accommodate a tool cabinet as large as 24 in. deep by 44 in. wide by 16 in. tall. The idea was to follow up that bench with this complementary, built-in tool cabinet.

As with all of my projects, I first drew the cabinet full scale in three views, including all the construction details I could think of.

Two boxes are better than one

I like the look of mitered corners and made that basic decision early on. Then I realized I wasn't very comfortable mitering an edge on a plywood panel nearly 4 ft. wide by only about 2 ft. long, so I decided to break the cabinet into two separate boxes. This makes the parts smaller and easier to handle, especially on the tablesaw. I also like the idea that if you have

Two cabinets are easier to build and move than a large one

The fact that this is a shop cabinet influenced many of the construction choices. Two separate boxes are easier to make than one big one. Plywood cabinets are joined with miters and splines and dressed up with solid-wood edge-banding and drawer fronts. Plywood drawer boxes get quick box joints, applied fronts, and commercial slides.

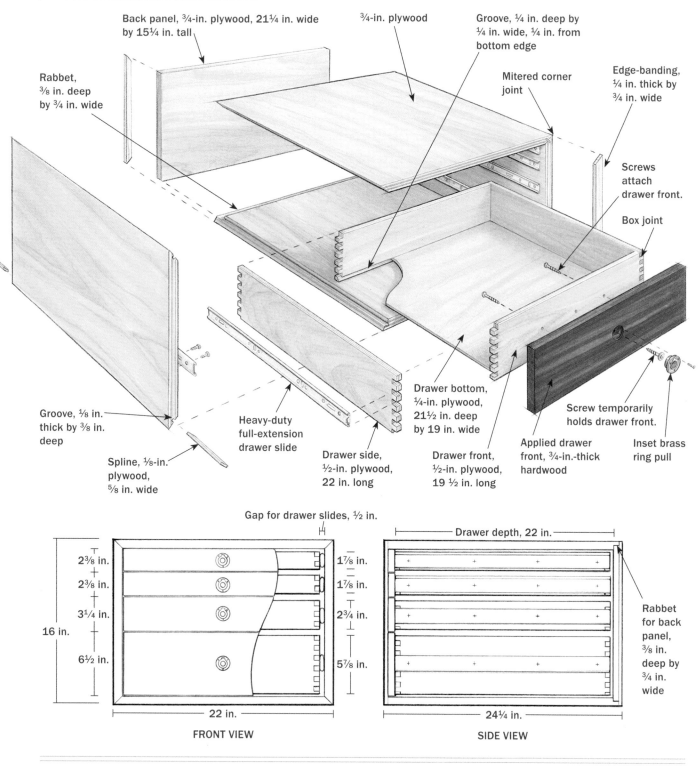

Back panel, ¾-in. plywood, 21¼ in. wide by 15¼ in. tall

¾-in. plywood

Groove, ¼ in. deep by ¼ in. wide, ¼ in. from bottom edge

Mitered corner joint

Edge-banding, ¼ in. thick by ¾ in. wide

Rabbet, ⅜ in. deep by ¾ in. wide

Screws attach drawer front.

Box joint

Groove, ⅛ in. thick by ⅜ in. deep

Spline, ⅛-in. plywood, ⅝ in. wide

Heavy-duty full-extension drawer slide

Drawer side, ½-in. plywood, 22 in. long

Drawer bottom, ¼-in. plywood, 21½ in. deep by 19 in. wide

Drawer front, ½-in. plywood, 19 ½ in. long

Applied drawer front, ¾-in.-thick hardwood

Screw temporarily holds drawer front.

Inset brass ring pull

Gap for drawer slides, ½ in.

2⅜ in.

2⅜ in.

3¼ in.

6½ in.

16 in.

22 in.

FRONT VIEW

1⅞ in.

1⅞ in.

2¾ in.

5⅞ in.

Drawer depth, 22 in.

24¼ in.

SIDE VIEW

Rabbet for back panel, ⅜ in. deep by ¾ in. wide

Miter the edges of the panels. Angle the sawblade just beyond 45 degrees to ensure tight corners. Sneak up on the final width, and then cut the rest of the parts to size.

Slot the edges for splines. Angle the sawblade at exactly 45 degrees and locate the grooves toward the fat corner of the edge.

Mitered plywood makes for quick box construction

The joinery is cut on the tablesaw, and packing tape draws the joints together tightly. For a utility cabinet like this, it is quicker to apply edge-banding after assembly.

CABINET JOINERY

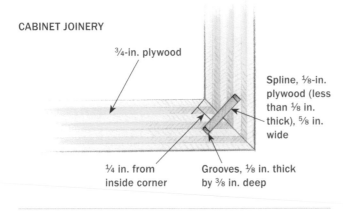

¾-in. plywood

Spline, ⅛-in. plywood (less than ⅛ in. thick), ⅝ in. wide

¼ in. from inside corner

Grooves, ⅛ in. thick by ⅜ in. deep

to break down your bench to move your shop, the two boxes will be manageable.

The workbench is maple, with walnut wedges in the trestle joinery. I like the visual contrast between these two woods, so I chose maple plywood for the carcases, and solid walnut for the drawer fronts.

To make sure the carcases would stand up to heavy use, I splined the miter joints and glued a full ¾-in.-thick panel into a rabbet in the back of each carcase. On the front and back edges of each box, I glued solid edge-banding to cover the plywood edges and splines.

I measured the heights of the tools I wanted to keep in the cabinet and discovered I needed more small drawers than large ones. I standardized the drawer sizes as much as I could so that I could make several parts of the same size. Your tools differ from mine, so size the drawers accordingly.

One sheet of ¾-in. maple plywood is plenty for the carcases. I used three 5×5 sheets of Baltic-birch plywood for the drawers, one ½ in. thick for the drawer sides and two ¼ in. thick for the bottoms.

Heavy-duty ball-bearing drawer slides offer smooth action and full extension, so they were an easy choice. I used Accuride® 3832 slides rated at 100 lb., which should be plenty strong, even when I pull out a drawer slightly to help support a wide board or panel held on edge in the front vise.

For drawer pulls, I chose inset brass ring pulls, which match the brass benchdogs and won't catch on cords.

Miter and spline the cabinet parts

Some folks might prefer to edge-band the plywood before cutting the miters and assembling the boxes, but I chose to do the edging afterward. This let me cut rabbets and spline slots all the way through on the tablesaw, because the front and back edges would be covered later. Also, the long miters had to be perfect only at their outermost edges.

The first step is to cut all the carcase pieces about 1 in. oversize, making sure the pieces are perfectly square. Next, mark the edges that get the miter cuts and rabbets: It is awfully easy to miter or rabbet the wrong edges.

Angle the tablesaw blade just a bit beyond 45 degrees to ensure that the outside, visible edges will be tight. If you cut four small sample pieces, you can use tape to wrap them into a box to check your miter angles. Use very flat plywood for all of the cabinet parts; if it is bowed it might lift off the saw table near the blade and the miters won't be accurate. Last, cut the rabbets for the backs.

Splines reinforce the miters

I used ⅛-in. plywood for the spline material, as it fits loosely into a single blade kerf. A loose fit, with glue, is enough to provide some insurance for the miter joints. If the fit is too tight, the splines will bind when inserted in the already-assembled box (see the bottom left photo). Angle the tablesaw blade at exactly 45 degrees for the spline cuts. When ripping the spline material to width, leave plenty of clearance in the slots.

Packing tape will be your clamps. For these large boxes, it is easiest to tape up pairs of panels at a time. To close the joints, pull on the tape as you apply it.

Two pairs of panels make a box. After spreading glue on the miters, stand up the panel assemblies and draw the last two joints together with more tape (above left). Apply glue to the spline stock and insert pieces roughly halfway into the joint (above right), working from both ends. Nail and glue the back panel into its rabbet, and trim the splines flush.

Tape is a great clamp for mitered boxes

You will insert the splines from the front and back after the boxes have been taped up, so cut the spline stock into halves lengthwise. A benefit of inserting the splines this way is that they force the excess glue into the center of the joint instead of out the front and back.

I assemble mitered boxes with stranded packing tape. Normally, I lay down the pieces in a line, outside face up, and run continuous strips of tape across all four sides, leaving a 4-in. or 5-in. tab at the end. When glue is applied and the pieces are wrapped up into a box, the tape puts firm, equalized pressure at the joints. In this case, however, I found the pieces too large to handle all at once, so I taped two panels at a time and assembled the box from there (see the photos on p. 49).

While the glue is wet, insert the splines and the back panels, which will square up the assemblies.

Edge-band the cases

Because you will apply the banding after these utility cabinets have been assembled, the easiest method is to make the edge-banding exactly as wide as the plywood is thick. It's not hard to apply it perfectly aligned with the edges.

Use the surface planer to bring the banding down to a final thickness of ¼ in. Take

Sturdy drawer box joints

Made quickly on the table-saw using a dado blade and crosscut jig, these finger joints create quick and strong drawer boxes. The drawer slides require an exact ½-in. gap on each side, so build a test drawer to dial in the final dimensions.

SIZING THE FINGERS

Start the ½-in.-wide fingers at the top edge and let them fall randomly at the bottom.

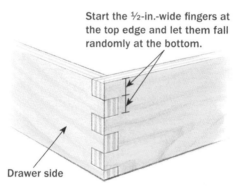

Drawer side

SUB-FENCE/JIG

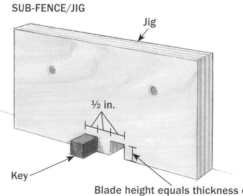

Jig

½ in.

Key

Blade height equals thickness of drawer sides plus ¹⁄₁₆ in.

The ends of each piece are identical. For the first cut, butt the top edge of the workpiece against the key.

Apply thin banding cut to exact width, using your fingers to align it. Dry-fit each piece first to fit the mitered ends. A 23-gauge micro-pinner leaves almost invisible holes.

Make the second cut. To cut the second notch, just place the first notch on the key. The final notch on this drawer will be partial.

Locating the mating side. Flip the first side, put its first notch on the key, and clamp it. Butt the mating side against the first side (above). Cut the first notch on the mating side (right). The dado blade should just clear the first side.

some pressure off yourself by making extra pieces. I used a nail gun to apply the edge-banding, using my fingertips to align it flush with the sides as I glued each piece (see the top photo on p. 51). A 23-gauge micro-pinner leaves almost invisible holes. Clamps or strips of masking tape can replace the nails, but you will need lots of them. Work your way around the edges of the cabinets, fitting and mitering each piece as you attach it.

Size the drawers carefully

In keeping with the practical nature of this project, I chose box-jointed (also called finger-jointed) drawer boxes with applied fronts. Box joints are strong, attractive, and easy to cut using a sled on the tablesaw. (For more information on cutting these joints, see "Sturdy drawer box joints" on pp. 50–51.)

The applied drawer fronts go on after the boxes are in place, making the fitting process much easier. In order for the drawer slides to work properly, it's important to have exactly ½ in. of space on either side of the drawer box. That's one reason to build the cabinet boxes first. Then, when cutting the drawer box joints, you must realize that raising or lowering the dado blade on the tablesaw will affect the size of the finished drawer box. Once you have set the blade height correctly, don't move it.

I run the box-joint fingers ¹⁄₁₆ in. extralong so that I can sand them flush after the drawer box is glued up. This means cutting the box parts ⅛ in. longer than I need them and carefully adjusting the blade height ¹⁄₁₆ in. above the thickness of the parts.

Install the drawer slides

Because these heavy-duty slides can be mounted anywhere on the drawer side, I was able to place them at the center and work from centerlines, which is my preference. After attaching the drawer slides to the drawer boxes, align and mount the other half of the slides inside the cases. To align the slides front to back, use a scrap of material equal to the thickness of the drawer fronts plus the recommended offset. To align the slides top to bottom, use a spacer panel placed under the slides, inside the cases, to be sure they are installed uniformly.

Initially, I installed the slides with only two screws. I got all the drawers installed and adjusted so that they worked properly, and then I inserted the rest of the screws.

Applied drawer fronts are easier to fit

Now comes the fun part: installing the solid-wood drawer fronts. The challenge is to have as fine and even a gap as possible around each drawer front, while allowing for some shrinking and swelling with changes in humidity. First, cut the drawer fronts to length and width so that they all fit together into the opening, with no gaps. With all of them in place, mark a centerline for the finger pulls, remove the fronts, and mortise for the pulls. All of the mortising is done easily on the drill press, with just a bit of chisel work afterward.

The mortises for these pulls allow a neat trick for attaching the fronts. Drill a clearance hole in the recess, through which you can loosely insert a pan-head screw. Now you can fit the drawer fronts one at a time, with the pan-head screws allowing some adjustment in all directions as you take light trimming cuts from the edges.

Once the fronts are in position, drive some screws into them from inside the drawer boxes to lock them in place. Then remove the pan-head screws and install the finger pulls.

Install the drawers

The drawer fronts are fit and applied after the slides and boxes are in place, making it easier to achieve fine, uniform gaps and a neat appearance.

A trick for installing slides. Working off the centerlines of the drawers and slides, use a spacer panel to set the distance between the slides and the cabinet bottom. A small block sets the distance from the front edge.

Fit and attach the drawer fronts. Drill a slightly oversize hole in the round mortise for a pan-head screw. Use credit cards to set the gaps, and use the screw to lock the drawer front in place. Then screw the front permanently from the inside, remove the temporary screw, and install the pull.

Finishing up

For these cabinets I applied the same finish I used on the bench: a few coats of varnish thinned about 50 percent with turpentine, applied with a rag and rubbed off before it dried. Last, I added a few thin cleats to the bottoms of the boxes, to keep them in place on the lower stretchers of the workbench.

Now everything is in its place. Sure, I can't remember which drawer my mortising chisel is in, but I know it's in there somewhere.

A Rock-Solid Plywood Bench

CECIL BRAEDEN

I had wanted to build a sturdy workbench for some time but was put off by the cost and complexity of a traditional hardwood bench. I knew that such benches derive much of their strength and rigidity from the mortises and tenons that join the framework, and I wondered if there was a way to combine this joinery with the inherent strength, rigidity, and dimensional accuracy of plywood. The design I created has a base of laminated sections of plywood and a top of plywood and medium-density fiberboard (MDF).

An advantage of this design is that the piece can be built without a planer or jointer, perfect for someone just getting started in woodworking. For under $250 including a vise, I have a bench with the rigidity I desired without breaking the bank.

Design the bench, create a cut plan, and begin

This method of construction can be adapted to almost any size and type of bench: You could even construct just the base and purchase a ready-made hardwood top. My bench is 33 in. wide by 72 in. long by 34 in. tall, a comfortable height for me to work at. It is also ⅛ in. lower than my tablesaw, allowing me to use the bench as an auxiliary outfeed table. The cut plan I used (see p. 57) allows you to create a bench with legs up to 36 in. long, giving a bench height of 37½ in.

All base components—legs, aprons, and stretchers—are laminations made from 3⁹⁄₁₆-in.-wide slats of ¾-in.-thick plywood. Set the tablesaw's fence and rip all the strips without changing the setting. You always will get some tearout when you cut plywood: This can be minimized with a zero-clearance insert on the tablesaw, but in any case rip with the show side of the plywood up. If you do get some tearout, lightly sand away any splinters and keep the tearout side inward when assembling the components.

The last step before laminating the components is to drill pocket holes every 6 in. on one side of the two outer apron pieces to attach the top with pocket screws. Or you can use the battens described on p. 60.

Glue-up requires quick work, attention to detail

Even with glue that has a moderate amount of open time, you must work quickly, so do a dry run first and have all components in order. I apply the glue to all mating surfaces with a disposable brush that has the bristles trimmed, but a roller would work. Glue the laminates on a flat surface protected by waxed paper.

Assemble and glue stretchers and aprons

Make sure all like pieces are trimmed to exactly the same length. Draw a line 3½ in.

Workbench dimensions

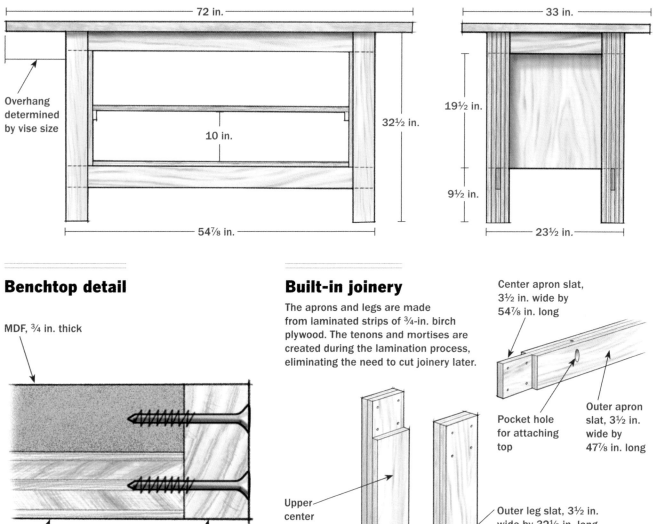

72 in.

Overhang determined by vise size

32½ in.

10 in.

54⅞ in.

33 in.

19½ in.

9½ in.

23½ in.

Benchtop detail

MDF, ¾ in. thick

Plywood, ¾ in. thick

Solid edging, ¾ in. thick

Built-in joinery

The aprons and legs are made from laminated strips of ¾-in. birch plywood. The tenons and mortises are created during the lamination process, eliminating the need to cut joinery later.

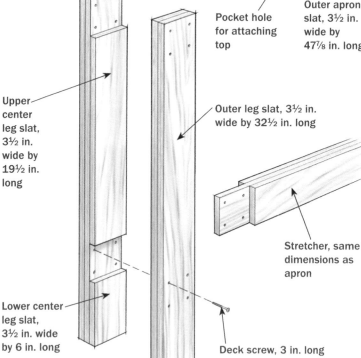

Center apron slat, 3½ in. wide by 54⅞ in. long

Pocket hole for attaching top

Outer apron slat, 3½ in. wide by 47⅞ in. long

Upper center leg slat, 3½ in. wide by 19½ in. long

Outer leg slat, 3½ in. wide by 32½ in. long

Stretcher, same dimensions as apron

Lower center leg slat, 3½ in. wide by 6 in. long

Deck screw, 3 in. long

Use cut plans to make the most of your plywood

If you decide to build a bench that is the same size as mine, or one that is slightly taller, use these cut plans. I used 2½ sheets of 4x8 birch plywood and a sheet of MDF from my local home center. Have your plywood seller make the first and second cuts as shown to ease handling the material.

Other materials needed are 2-, 2½-, and 3-in.-long deck screws, and a quart of fresh PVA woodworking glue. I've used both Titebond® II and III, but particularly in hot, dry conditions, glues with extended open times make alignment of the laminations easier.

Outer leg slats

Upper center leg slats

Outer apron/stretcher slats

Waste used for assembly jigs

First cut

22½ in.

Outer apron/stretcher slats

Center apron/stretcher slats

Outer leg slats

First cut

23½ in.

BENCHTOP
The top consists of a layer of ¾-in. plywood topped with ¾-in. MDF.

End

End

Second cut

15 in.

Outer leg slats

Outer leg slats

Spare slat

Spare slat

Lower center leg slats

Spacers for leg glue-ups

Upper shelf

Lower shelf

The two optional shelves come out of a half sheet of ¾-in.-thick plywood.

from both ends of the longer center-slat pieces, and mark the ends of both sides with an "X" to indicate non-glue areas. If you are using pocket holes on the aprons, make sure the holes are facing outward and upward.

Glue the three pieces of each component together, being careful not to get any glue on the tenon ends. Turn the assembly on edge so that the plies are facing up and insert one end in the apron jig (see drawing below). As you apply clamping pressure, keep the slats aligned and pushed against the jig to maintain the

3½-in. tenon and even cheeks. When the glue is dry, run both exposed-ply sides of each component through the tablesaw to clean them up.

Next, make the legs

Prior to assembly, make the spacer blocks (see photos on the facing page) and wrap about 5 in. of each with clear tape. Used to create the lower mortise on each leg, the spacer is driven out after the leg has dried. Tape prevents glue from sticking to the spacer. The leg stack consists of two outside slats, the lower center piece, the spacer, the upper center piece, and two more outside slats. Locate the upper and lower mortise areas and mark both mating surfaces so that you will remember not to apply glue there.

Construct the aprons and stretchers. These parts consist of a center strip of plywood that includes the two tenons, and two shorter outer strips that form the shoulders of the tenon. Have multiple clamps ready for use.

A simple jig aids apron assembly

When gluing the stretchers and aprons, use a jig to align the center slat at the proper offset to create the tenon.

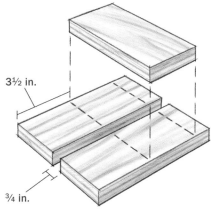

3½ in.

¾ in.

Gluing the legs

To assemble the legs of your workbench, first insert a taped spacer block to hold open the lower mortise. An L-shaped jig keeps the sections aligned. Use a generous amount of glue, but don't apply glue to those areas that face the spacer block (photo 1).

When the sections have been glued together, turn the assembly upward and apply the clamps. Waxed paper protects the work surface (photo 2). When the glue has dried, knock out the taped spacer block with a mallet and a thin piece of wood to reveal the mortise (photo 3).

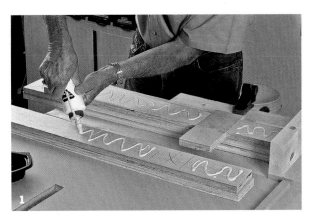

A simple L-shaped jig helps to lay up the legs accurately. Glue the slats together, remembering to insert the spacer. After assembly, turn the stack so that the spacer is sticking up. Using both sides of the jig, keep the ends and edges of each slat in perfect alignment and the center slats pressed tightly against the spacer as you apply clamping pressure. Apply two small clamps to both outside pairs of slats that form the upper mortise.

After the glue has set, make cleanup cuts on the tablesaw. Use sandpaper to slightly chamfer the bottom edges of the finished legs to prevent splintering of the outer veneer if the bench is dragged across the floor.

Clean up the edges. After the legs, aprons, and stretchers have been assembled, run both edges past a sawblade to clean up glue residue and leave them at the final 3½-in. width. Cut the first edges with the fence at 3⁹⁄₁₆ in. and the opposite edges at 3½ in.

Assemble the frame sides, then join them with plywood panels

Start by dry-fitting the tenon on each end of a stretcher into its respective mortise. If a tenon extends beyond the leg, trim it flush or slightly recessed. Lay a leg on a flat surface protected with waxed paper. Apply glue to the mortise-and-tenon, then insert the tenon and clamp lightly. Use a carpenter's square to bring the stretcher and leg to exactly 90 degrees (photo 1, on the facing page), and tighten the clamp. Remove the excess glue with a damp cloth, put the joint aside to set, and assemble the second leg and stretcher.

Once the glue has set, remove the clamps and lay the leg/stretcher down with the inside facing up. Drill four countersunk pilot holes at least 2½ in. deep into each joint and drive in waxed 3-in. deck screws. Reinforcing the joints in this manner may not be necessary, but it is very cheap insurance that the joints will hold forever.

Stand the assembly on the floor with the stretcher pointing up. Place waxed paper under the apron mortise; apply glue to the mortise and insert an apron tenon, being sure the pocket holes are oriented properly. Check for 90 degrees and clamp the apron with a bar clamp. When the joint is dry, reinforce it with screws and then attach the other leg in the same manner.

The benchtop should rest on the aprons, not the legs, so if the top of a leg is higher than the apron tenon, trim it flush. Sand the exposed joints on the legs to remove glue residue.

If you are not using pocket screws to attach the top, prepare a couple of 2-in.-square battens with countersunk holes in two directions. Clamp the battens flush with the top inside edge of the aprons and attach them with 3-in. deck screws.

Stand the front and rear assemblies on their legs on a level floor, and cut two pieces of plywood to fit between the stretchers and aprons and to the desired width of the frame. These sides will serve as the end stretchers. There will be space to install an end vise above the side of the bench if desired. Chamfer the edges of the sides. Drill countersunk holes every 3 in., 1¾ in. in from both edges to locate the screws in the center ply of the legs. Clamp the sides in place with the edges flush with the outside edges of the legs. Be sure to check that the frame is square by measuring the diagonal between opposite corners; adjust until the distances are even, then tighten the clamps. Now drill pilot holes 1½ in. deep through the previously drilled countersunk holes, and drive 2½-in. deck screws (photo 3, on the facing page).

Next, add two plywood shelves, the lower one attached to the front and rear stretchers with 2-in. screws and the upper one screwed to battens attached with 3-in. screws through the end stretchers into the legs. Because the shelves, sides, and top are screwed on, the whole bench can be disassembled for moving.

Make and attach the top

If you are making your own top, lay the layers upside down, making sure one end of the assembly is flush, and screw them together using countersunk screws that will not go through the top layer. Cut the other sides flush using a circular saw and straightedge or the tablesaw.

Ask a friend to help place the top on the frame and position as desired. Mark the corners of the legs on the underside of the top. Then turn the top over and mark the holes for the vise(s) on the bottom side so that you can drill small holes through. You may have to add a spacer block to bring the vise jaws level with the top. Turn the top back over and use a spade bit to drill recesses for the bolt heads at each of the small holes. Then drill for the bolts and attach the vise.

At this point you can attach the top: Place it on the bench frame and secure it with the pocket holes or battens.

To protect the soft edge of the MDF top, I screwed a solid wood edging around the entire benchtop, leaving a gap for the vise.

Drill holes for benchdogs (if desired), and you are done. If you plan to use this bench primarily for glue-ups or finishing, a good choice would be to laminate the top; otherwise, apply a clear finish or just leave it natural.

Assembling the base

Begin with the frame sides when assembling the base of your workbench. Insert the stretcher and apron into the leg, making sure they meet at exactly 90 degrees (photo 1). Reinforce the joints with four 3-in. deck screws. With the side frame resting on the floor, add the second leg (photo 2). Finally, add the plywood end stretchers (photo 3). Clamp them in place, check the base for squareness, then attach with screws.

A Heavy-Duty Workbench

MIKE DUNBAR

This is my workbench. Two friends and I each made one like it in the mid-1970s, copying a 200-year-old original we found in the basement of an 18th-century mansion. I prefer it to any other design, for several reasons. The bench is a heavy, solid structure. No matter how hard the work, there is no need to hold down this one with sandbags. And its joints don't wobble when I'm handplaning or sawing. If they do loosen because of seasonal movement, a tweak with a bed-bolt wrench makes them rigid again.

The bench's wood vises are very strong. The twin-screw front vise has ample space between the screws, which means I can drop a long, wide part between them. And the jaws are wide enough to hold a 6-ft.-long board for edge-jointing without additional support.

The bench does not have a tool tray, leaving its entire wide top available not just for woodworking but also for assembly. When I worked by myself as a professional furniture maker, this bench was all I needed. Finally, I am a woodworker, and a bench made entirely of wood has a deep appeal for me.

Making this bench is more heavy work than it is hard, although the tail vise is somewhat complicated. Many of the parts are so large that joining them borders on timber framing. A second pair of hands comes in handy for some stages on the project.

Some heavy lifting will be required

The bench can be made of just about any type of hardwood. Because this is a workbench, practicality governed my choices. In my region, yellow birch is cheaper than maple but isn't available above 10/4. So I used birch for the 2-in.-thick parts and hard maple for the thicker ones. If you cannot find 12/4 hardwood, you can glue up your stock.

Before cutting any wood, determine what bench height is comfortable for you. When working with hand tools, it is more efficient and easier if you can bring into play all of the larger muscle groups in your body, above all those in your legs and back. Most benches are too high for me, forcing me to work only with my shoulders and arms. I am 5 ft. 9 in. and a little short in the leg. My benchtop is 32 in. high.

Besides wood, you will need to order two other items: 1¾-in.-dia. wooden bench screws and threaded blocks, which you can get from Crystal Creek Mill (P.O. Box 41, DeWitt, NY 13214; 315-446-1229).

You can cut your own threads if you have a large tap and die suited for this job (one that's at least 1½ in. dia. with 5 tpi or fewer). Antique tap-and-die sets for wood may be found at flea markets or tag sales. The tap would be the most useful of the two, because it would allow you to make the threaded end batten near the tail vise out of one piece of wood.

A heavy-duty bench with a wide top, knockdown base, and large vises

Square threaded blocks are sold with vise screws; angle sides for mechanical strength.

Garters, 5/16 in. thick by 1 7/8 in. wide by 1 3/4 in. tall, fit into groove in vise screws.

Clearance dadoes for vise screws, 1 3/4 in. deep by 2 in. wide

Plywood is screwed into 3/4-in.-deep by 1-in.-wide rabbet.

Support cleat, 1 1/4 in. thick by 2 in. wide by 10 in. long

End batten, 1 3/4 in. thick by 2 3/4 in. wide by 30 1/4 in. long

Bed bolts attach end batten to plank and cleat.

Captured nut

Back legs, 3 in. thick by 4 in. wide by 31 1/2 in. long, including 1-in. by 3-in. by 3/4-in. tenon

Side stretchers, 3 in. thick by 4 in. wide by 21 5/8 in. long, including 1-in. by 4-in. by 1 1/4-in. tenon

Front legs, 3 in. thick by 4 in. wide by 30 in. long, including 1-in. by 3-in. by 1 1/4-in. tenon

Bed bolts, 3/8 in. dia. by 6 in. long

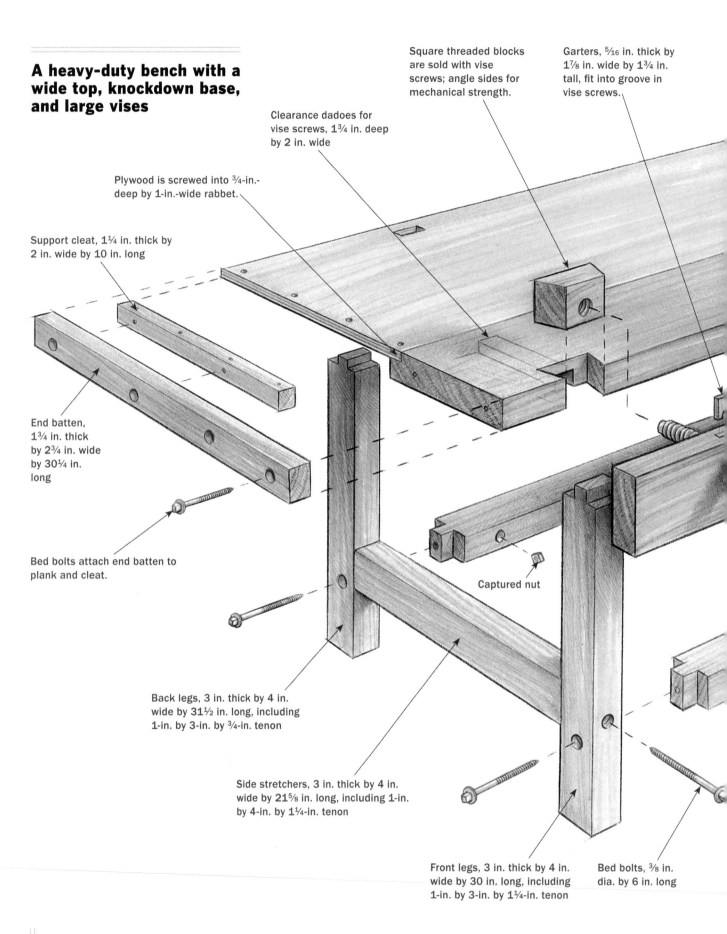

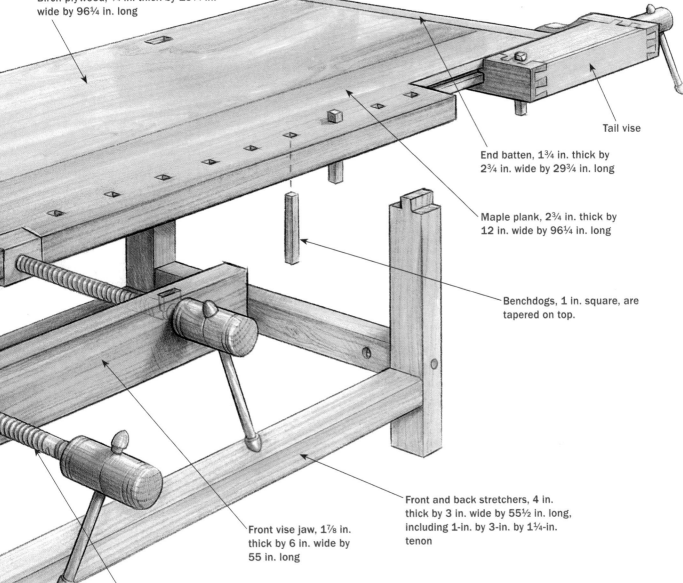

Birch plywood, ¾ in. thick by 19¼ in. wide by 96¼ in. long

Tail vise

End batten, 1¾ in. thick by 2¾ in. wide by 29¾ in. long

Maple plank, 2¾ in. thick by 12 in. wide by 96¼ in. long

Benchdogs, 1 in. square, are tapered on top.

Front and back stretchers, 4 in. thick by 3 in. wide by 55½ in. long, including 1-in. by 3-in. by 1¼-in. tenon

Front vise jaw, 1⅞ in. thick by 6 in. wide by 55 in. long

1¾-in. dia. wood screw, 2½ tpi

Without it you'll have to join one of the threaded blocks to the end of the batten. The Beall Tool Co. (www.bealltool.com) offers wood-threading kits for making 1½-in.-dia., 5-tpi screws and nuts. It includes a router jig and bit and a 1½-in.-dia. tap, which would solve the aforementioned joinery problem.

You'll also need 16 bed bolts and a wrench, which you can get from Ball and Ball Hardware Reproductions (www.ballandball-us.com).

A knockdown base is easy to move

The original bench knocks down completely. This leads me to suspect that it belonged to an interior joiner, what we would call today a finish carpenter. These guys were the elite of the building tradesmen and were responsible for raised-panel walls, wainscoting, staircases, mantels, moldings, and doors.

Base and benchtop

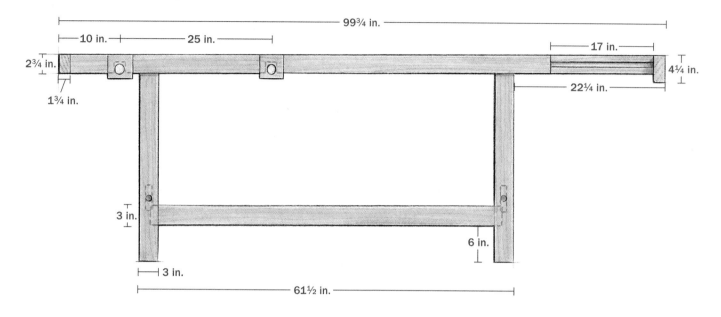

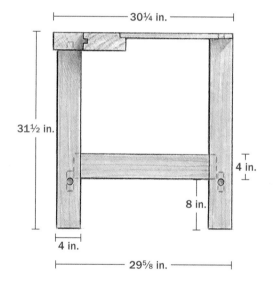

Working on a magnificent Portsmouth, N.H., mansion, a joiner could be on the job site for months. He would move his bench and toolbox right into the house. When finished, he'd put them in a wagon and move them onto the next job site. A bench that knocks down is still a good idea today because it is easier to move to a new shop.

The legs and stretchers are joined with mortises and tenons held together with bed bolts. The joints can't be at the same height or the bed bolts would bump each other, so offset their elevations. Notice that there are tenons on the tops of the legs, as well, to secure the top to the base. Cut all of the joints at the same time.

Cut the shoulders of these large tenons with a circular saw and then rip the cheeks on the bandsaw. Bore out the mortises with a drill bit and square the corners with a chisel. I used a shoulder plane to fit the tenons.

Bed-bolt basics

Bed bolts are very effective fasteners and, when tightened, will not allow the slightest wiggle. The bolt has a square head with a large flange and requires a two-step hole. Drill the counterbore for the flange first. The long hole for the bolt goes into the bottom of the mortise, through the length of the tenon and past the location of the nut.

The nut sits in a hole drilled into the back of the rail. Assembling the joint is easy: Tap the mortise and tenon together, hold the nut in place and slide a bed bolt into the hole. A couple of quick turns catches the nut. When all of the fasteners are hand-tight, grab the bed-bolt wrench and finish the job.

The plank is the key to the top

The top of the bench is made of two pieces: a 3-in.-thick plank at the front and a thinner plywood panel behind. The front and back legs are different heights as a result. The thick front plank anchors the vises and provides a durable surface for your heaviest and most forceful work. The rear panel will not take the same punishment as the front and does not have to be as thick. Its role is to provide a wide, level surface. On the original bench this was a wide pine board, but I used birch plywood for its stability.

The width of the front plank is a variable and can depend on whatever you can find or glue up. A piece of wood this thick is seldom flat as it comes from the lumber dealer and will need to be planed. If your machines are not up to a job this heavy, you may have to find someone who can do the work for you. I surfaced my 12-in.-wide plank in my planer, because it wouldn't fit on my jointer. Luckily it was straight but just cupped a bit. I took a couple of passes off the domed (heart) side, just to get a flat surface to work on. Then, I took light passes off the concave side. Because this surface is not seen, there is no need to flatten it completely. Finally, I flipped the plank again and finished dressing the upper surface. Set the plank aside for several days

Timber-frame techniques.
Use a circular saw to cut the tenon shoulders on these large beams. The cheeks are then cut on the bandsaw. Get an assistant, if you can find one, to help you support the long, heavy timbers. For the mortises in the legs, first drill out the waste, then square with a chisel. Afterward, the tenons are pared to fit the mortises.

and let it equalize before flattening it again with a light pass. While you are at it, joint the front edge so that it is straight and square to the upper surface.

This plank requires a few operations before it's ready to drop into place on the substructure. First, lay out the leg mortises in the underside and cut and fit them to the tenons on the top of the front legs. Next, rout the rabbet in the back edge to create a lip that will support the plywood portion of the top, which will be secured with wood screws.

Make room for the vises

The front vise is secured to the bench with wood screws threaded through two dovetail-shaped nuts, which are set into the plank. Bevel the sides of two of the three threaded blocks (the other one is for the tail-vise assembly). Then use the blocks to lay out

their recesses. Lay out these notches so that the blocks project slightly from the front edge of the benchtop; plane them flush later. Cut the deep notches with a handsaw or circular saw, and clean up the walls with a wide chisel.

The top is far too thick for the wood screws to clear it on the bottom side, so you have to cut channels for clearance. Tap the nuts into place temporarily to see where the threaded holes line up with the bench. Cut the channel edges first, with a straightedge clamped on the plank to guide your circular saw. Then make a lot of kerf cuts through the center and chop out the waste.

Now you can glue in the threaded nuts. Leave the tops slightly proud and plane them flush after the glue is dry. Plane the front edges flush, too. Next, cut out the large notch for the tail vise. A circular saw will cut through

Locate the leg mortises on the plank. First turn everything upside down and level the back legs.

Size and strength. The thick wooden screws are far enough apart to accommodate a wide workpiece, and the jaw is long enough to support a 6-ft. board for edge-jointing.

After angling the sides of the threaded blocks, lay out their recesses. The trapezoidal shape gives mechanical strength to this joint, which is also glued.

Circular saw comes in handy again. Cut the shoulders first, then cut some kerfs through the waste section.

After chopping out the waste, pare the sides. Use one of the threaded blocks to guide your chisel.

most of the stock, but you will need a handsaw to complete the corner. Clean up the sawcuts with a handplane, keeping everything square (not the easiest task but very important). Rout the long groove along the notch, and finish it with a sharp chisel.

The last task in preparing the front plank is to cut the dog holes. Although you can use any type of dog you prefer, I chose the clever, low-tech type I found on the original. The dog holes are ⅞ in. square, and each square dog has a slight taper planed onto one face. There is a dog for each hole in the bench. Each is tapped into place from below, narrowside up, and sits flush with the top until it is needed. Tap it with a mallet until it projects slightly above the surface and tightens in place. The dog holes are roughly 6½ in. apart, but some are offset to avoid the screws for the front vise.

End battens support the plywood portion of the benchtop. Each batten is bolted to the thick plank and also to a cleat that supports the plywood and keeps it level with the plank. The plywood is screwed onto the cleat and into a rabbet at the back edge of the plank.

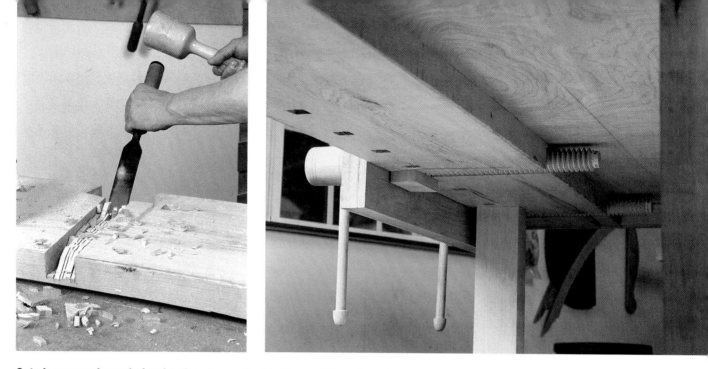

Cut clearance channels for the vise screws. Tap the threaded blocks into place temporarily to determine the location of these channels. Remove the blocks before cutting. Define the edges with a circular saw, kerf out the middle, then chop out the waste.

The plywood section

The bench's end battens are bed-bolted to the thick plank and have support cleats along their inside edges for securing the plywood. The plywood is also screwed into the rabbet on the back edge of the thick plank (bottom photo, p. 69). With the thick plank in place on the front legs, place the plywood in its rabbet to locate the mortises for the rear legs. Cut these mortises, then attach the plywood to the plank and the end battens.

A trick for vise handles

Each wood screw has a thick hub with lines scribed into it. These are both for decoration and for laying out the holes for the handles. Drill a 1-in.-dia. hole. You can make the handles out of a piece of dowel with pins in the ends or end caps to keep them from falling out. However, I prefer the old technology used by the original maker. Turn your handles using wood that is still slightly green. You can split some from a firewood pile. Leave the ends ⅛ in. bigger than the hole in the vise-screw hub.

Boil one of the bullet-shaped ends to soften it, and drive it through the hub with a mallet. The wood will compress as it passes through the hole (some may be sheared away by the hole's edges), then it will spring back on the other side.

Front vise jaw wears a garter

The jaw is a piece of 8/4 hardwood. Its width is not critical and can depend on the wood you have on hand. Unlike most period benches I have examined, in which the user has to pull the vise jaw backward after loosening the screws, the jaw on this bench has garters that mate with a groove in the screws and keep the jaw and screws moving together.

Drill the two holes in the jaw for the wooden screws. Then cut the slots for the garters. Make the garters out of hardwood. One at a time, place a screw through the jaw and tap the garter into place. Turn the screws

A garter keeps the vise jaw moving with the screw. This thin strip is mortised into the jaw and fits into a groove near the screw hub.

Think of the tail vise as a three-sided box with closed ends. Build up the jaw end (foreground) from thinner stock. An ogee contour decorates the opposite end piece. The top, side, and bottom are joined to the ends with large dovetails.

Slide the assembled tail vise into place to locate the holes for the vise screw. This measurement determines where the vise screw will pass through the end of the tail vise and where it will enter the jaw end (below).

to test the fit of the garters. Before gluing them into place, be sure they aren't rubbing too tightly against the screw.

Tail vise is the tough part

The tail vise and its associated assembly make for some complicated joinery. A lot is going on at one time as the vise travels. The batten that stiffens the end of the benchtop and holds the front plank and plywood level is threaded for the tail-vise screw. It also acts as one of the guides for the vise. Without a large tap to cut the threads in the batten, I had to find a way to join one of the threaded blocks to it. I settled on a version of a scarf joint that provides some mechanical support and plenty of glue surface.

The vise itself is a three-sided box with closed ends. The jaw end is a 4-in.-square piece of hardwood. I glued up mine in a sandwich from thinner stock, which made it easier to create the tongue that protrudes from this block. A hole in the inside surface of the jaw receives the end of the vise screw.

Tail vise

This complex-looking unit is basically a three-sided box that slides back and forth on the tip of the bench's end batten. One wrinkle: The threaded nut included with the screw set must be joined to the end batten.

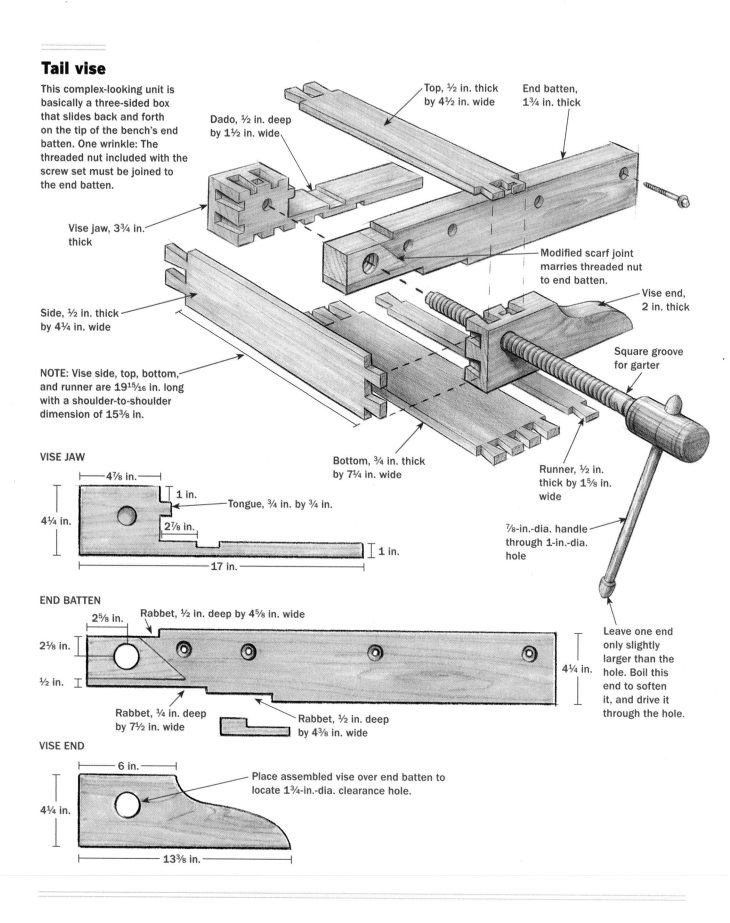

Top, ½ in. thick by 4½ in. wide

End batten, 1¾ in. thick

Dado, ½ in. deep by 1½ in. wide

Vise jaw, 3¾ in. thick

Modified scarf joint marries threaded nut to end batten.

Side, ½ in. thick by 4¼ in. wide

Vise end, 2 in. thick

Square groove for garter

NOTE: Vise side, top, bottom, and runner are 19¹⁵⁄₁₆ in. long with a shoulder-to-shoulder dimension of 15⅜ in.

Bottom, ¾ in. thick by 7¼ in. wide

Runner, ½ in. thick by 1⅝ in. wide

⅞-in.-dia. handle through 1-in.-dia. hole

VISE JAW

4⅞ in.

1 in.

Tongue, ¾ in. by ¾ in.

4¼ in.

2⅞ in.

1 in.

17 in.

END BATTEN

Rabbet, ½ in. deep by 4⅝ in. wide

2⅝ in.

2⅛ in.

½ in.

4¼ in.

Rabbet, ¼ in. deep by 7½ in. wide

Rabbet, ½ in. deep by 4⅜ in. wide

Leave one end only slightly larger than the hole. Boil this end to soften it, and drive it through the hole.

VISE END

6 in.

Place assembled vise over end batten to locate 1¾-in.-dia. clearance hole.

4¼ in.

13⅜ in.

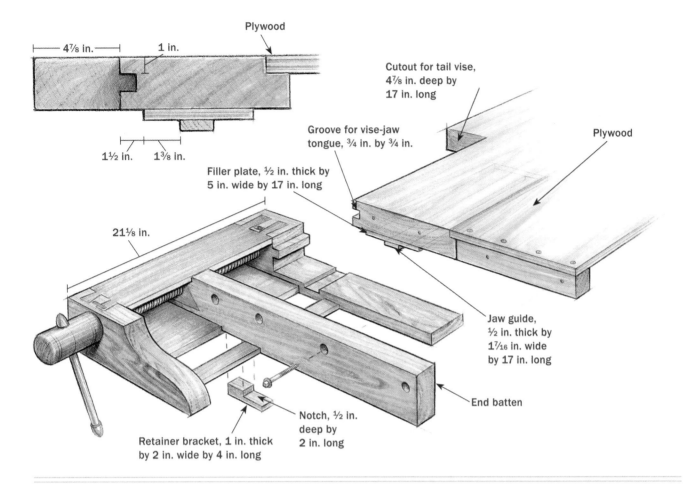

Plywood

|← 4⅞ in. →| 1 in.

1½ in. 1⅜ in.

21⅛ in.

Cutout for tail vise,
4⅞ in. deep by
17 in. long

Groove for vise-jaw
tongue, ¾ in. by ¾ in.

Plywood

Filler plate, ½ in. thick by
5 in. wide by 17 in. long

Jaw guide,
½ in. thick by
1⁷⁄₁₆ in. wide
by 17 in. long

End batten

Retainer bracket, 1 in. thick
by 2 in. wide by 4 in. long

Notch, ½ in.
deep by
2 in. long

The other end piece is 8/4 and has a clearance hole drilled through it for the screw. The ogee contour on this piece is more decorative than functional.

The top and side pieces of this box are ½ in. thick and joined to the jaw with large half-blind dovetails. The bottom is ¾ in. thick and joined the same way. There also is a guide strip on the bottom, which is ½ in. thick and also dovetailed to the jaw and end pieces. Make all of the parts for the tail vise, then test their fit and action before glue-up (see the center and bottom photos, p. 71).

Cut the mortise for the garter and tap it into place. You cannot avoid cutting into the dovetails when you make this mortise. Drill and square the dog hole in the jaw the same

way as those in the benchtop. This hole should fit between the dovetails.

Use bed bolts to secure the end batten to the thick part of the benchtop. Make the small retainer bracket through which the narrow guide strip passes and screw it into place on the end batten.

The vise may work somewhat stiffly at first but will eventually wear in so that it moves smoothly and without effort. Waxing the moving surfaces will help the action.

I completed my bench by finishing it with several coats of boiled linseed oil thinned with a little turpentine. Let the wood absorb as much oil as possible before wiping off the excess.

A Bench Built to Last

DICK MCDONOUGH

Built to last. This workbench has a wide top and a sturdy base
that provides solid footing and plenty of storage space.

If this workbench played football, I'm certain it would be a lineman. Because, like the guards and tackles found on the gridiron, my bench is big and solid. And I wouldn't have it any other way.

Most of my work involves the fabrication of large case goods—entertainment centers, bookcases, and other types of storage furniture. And although much of the machine work gets done using a tablesaw and router, I still do a good deal of work at the bench. So when it was time to replace my older, smallish, and somewhat rickety workbench, I opted to make a new one with all the bells and whistles. The bench would provide plenty of size and sturdiness. Sturdiness is the operative word here. Indeed, no matter how aggressive I get with a saw, a handplane, or a mallet and chisel, the bench doesn't wobble. The result is a workbench that has just about everything I need.

The supersized top is another important feature. With about 22 sq. ft. of surface area, the top is great for supporting long boards and wide sheet goods. Two end vises, a front vise, and a shoulder vise, along with a small army of benchdog holes, make it easy to secure almost any size stock to the bench.

My bench is considered left-handed, based on the location of the shoulder vise. If you prefer a right-handed bench, just build the shoulder vise on the right side.

The base creates a sturdy foundation

The bench owes much of its sturdiness to the design of the base. Yet its construction is pretty straightforward. It has just five main parts: three support frames and a pair of boxes. Screwing the frames and boxes together creates a single, rock-solid unit that can accept almost any kind of top. And the two boxes provide a ton of space for adding cabinets or drawers.

Front vise is nice. Used in conjunction with round benchdogs, the front vise lets the author work comfortably from the end of the bench.

Shoulder vise adds clamping options. The lack of a vise screw between the jaw surfaces makes the shoulder vise especially handy when a board must be clamped vertically.

Drawers galore. The shallow top drawer provides a perfect place for the author to store his favorite chisels.

The center and right-side support frames are identical. But to provide additional support for the shoulder vise, the left-side support frame is longer and has an extra leg. I added seven heavy-duty levelers—one under each leg of the support frame.

To simplify the construction of the base, I made both plywood boxes the same size. They fit snugly between the top rail and the foot of the frames, which adds rigidity to the base. If you include drawers in one of the boxes, as I did, cut the dadoes for the drawer-support cleats, then glue the cleats into the dadoes before the box is assembled.

Once the support frames and boxes were put together, I was able to assemble the base without much fuss. The boxes butt against the legs, with the bottom of the boxes simply resting on the narrow lip along the length of the foot. Attaching the boxes to the frames was a matter of driving five wood screws through the inside of the box into each of the legs.

Once the base was built, I moved it to its final location. Next I leveled the top surface using winding sticks and the seven levelers. Then I was ready to build the top right on the base.

A massive top on a sturdy modular base

To help keep costs under control, the top is a hybrid, a mix of solid maple, thick veneer, and particleboard. The base construction is surprisingly simple—a pair of plywood boxes sandwiched between three frames—yet the single unit that results is as solid as a '72 Buick.

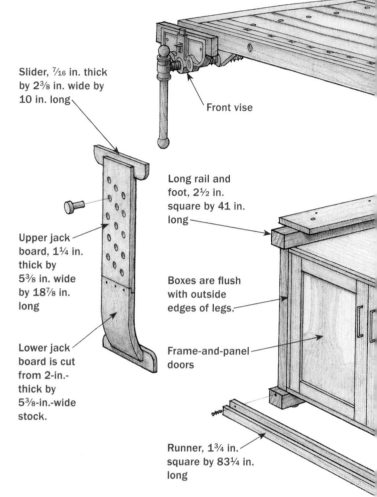

Slider, 7/16 in. thick by 2 3/8 in. wide by 10 in. long

Front vise

Upper jack board, 1 1/4 in. thick by 5 3/8 in. wide by 18 7/8 in. long

Lower jack board is cut from 2-in.-thick by 5 3/8-in.-wide stock.

Long rail and foot, 2 1/2 in. square by 41 in. long

Boxes are flush with outside edges of legs.

Frame-and-panel doors

Runner, 1 3/4 in. square by 83 1/4 in. long

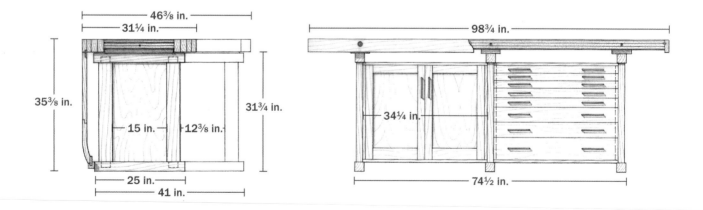

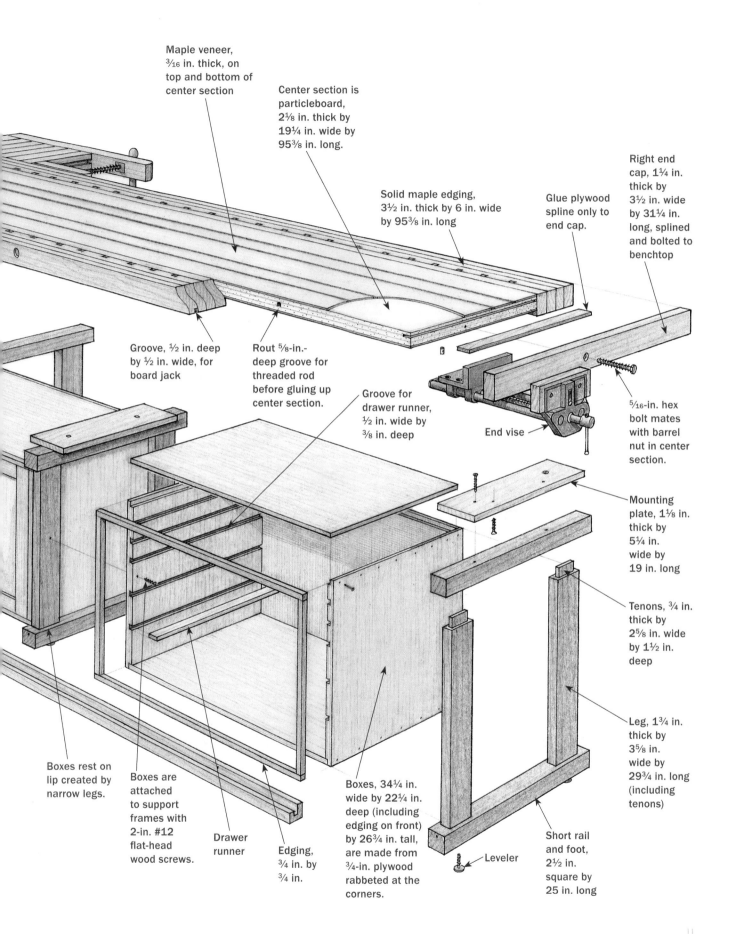

Maple veneer, 3/16 in. thick, on top and bottom of center section

Center section is particleboard, 2⅛ in. thick by 19¼ in. wide by 95⅜ in. long.

Solid maple edging, 3½ in. thick by 6 in. wide by 95⅜ in. long

Glue plywood spline only to end cap.

Right end cap, 1¼ in. thick by 3½ in. wide by 31¼ in. long, splined and bolted to benchtop

Groove, ½ in. deep by ½ in. wide, for board jack

Rout ⅝-in.-deep groove for threaded rod before gluing up center section.

Groove for drawer runner, ½ in. wide by ⅜ in. deep

End vise

5/16-in. hex bolt mates with barrel nut in center section.

Mounting plate, 1⅛ in. thick by 5¼ in. wide by 19 in. long

Tenons, ¾ in. thick by 2⅝ in. wide by 1½ in. deep

Boxes rest on lip created by narrow legs.

Boxes are attached to support frames with 2-in. #12 flat-head wood screws.

Drawer runner

Edging, ¾ in. by ¾ in.

Boxes, 34¼ in. wide by 22¼ in. deep (including edging on front) by 26¾ in. tall, are made from ¾-in. plywood rabbeted at the corners.

Leveler

Short rail and foot, 2½ in. square by 25 in. long

Leg, 1¾ in. thick by 3⅝ in. wide by 29¾ in. long (including tenons)

Shoulder vise and end cap

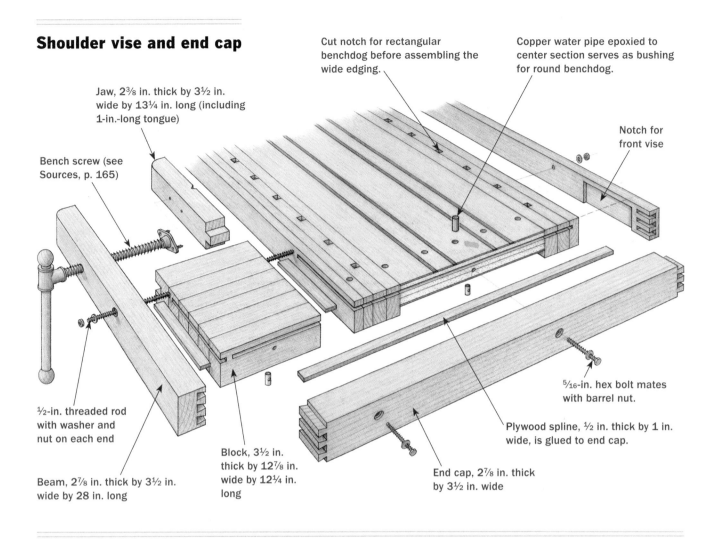

Jaw, 2⅜ in. thick by 3½ in. wide by 13¼ in. long (including 1-in.-long tongue)

Cut notch for rectangular benchdog before assembling the wide edging.

Copper water pipe epoxied to center section serves as bushing for round benchdog.

Notch for front vise

Bench screw (see Sources, p. 165)

½-in. threaded rod with washer and nut on each end

Beam, 2⅞ in. thick by 3½ in. wide by 28 in. long

Block, 3½ in. thick by 12⅞ in. wide by 12¼ in. long

End cap, 2⅞ in. thick by 3½ in. wide

Plywood spline, ½ in. thick by 1 in. wide, is glued to end cap.

5/16-in. hex bolt mates with barrel nut.

The top is flat and durable

The top has three main parts. There's a center section made from veneered particleboard. Attached to the center section are two 6-in.-wide edgings—one in front, the other in back—both made from glued-up solid maple.

Start with the center section

To help keep costs under control, I face-glued three pieces of particleboard together—a ⅝-in.-thick piece sandwiched between two ¾-in.-thick pieces.

First, I joined one of the ¾-in.-thick pieces to the ⅝-in.-thick piece, making sure all of the edges were flush. Then, I used a ⅝-in.-dia. core-box bit to cut three ⅝-in.-deep grooves across the underside of the ⅝-in.-thick particleboard. When the remaining piece of particleboard was added, the groove produced a ⅝-in. semicircular hole, which accommodated a threaded rod that helps secure the solid-maple edgings.

A workbench top gets a lot of wear and tear, so I used a 3/16-in.-thick veneer on top. And to make sure any movement stresses would be equal, I also veneered the bottom.

To make the veneer, I resawed maple to about a 5/16-in. thickness on the bandsaw. I used a thickness planer to bring the material to final thickness. Then I jointed one edge of each piece of veneer and ripped the other edge parallel on the tablesaw.

At this point, the veneer was ready to be applied to the particleboard. But faced with having to veneer such a large surface with thick veneer and without a lot of clamps, I used a somewhat unusual gluing-and-clamping technique (see "Gluing thick veneer to a large surface," on p. 80).

Wide edgings accept benchdogs

The wide edgings that run along the front and back of the bench are made of solid maple. That way the benchdogs have plenty of support when in use.

I routed the dadoes that create the openings for the rectangular-shaped benchdogs before the pieces were glued together.

I also wanted benchdogs to work with the front vise. But it was going to be a hassle to chop out all of those square mortises with a chisel. Plus, the particleboard wouldn't hold up well when the dogs got squeezed. So I opted to use round benchdogs. That way I simply had to bore a hole to accept it. And to reinforce the particleboard, I glued a short length of ¾-in. copper water pipe into the hole.

Three lengths of ½-in.-dia. threaded rod, with a washer and nut on each end, secure the wide, solid-maple edgings to the veneered center section. The rods extend through the "holes" in the particleboard and into through-holes in the edgings.

To drill the through-holes, I first cut each piece of edging to final length. Then to mark the location of the holes in the edgings, I clamped one piece to the center section. I made a center-point marker by driving a finish nail in the end of a long, ½-in.-dia. dowel. The nail must be centered in the end. I ran the dowel through the holes in the particleboard and used the nail to mark the center point of the hole in the edging. Once all of the points were marked, I drilled all of the holes through each piece of edging.

The threaded rod closest to the left end is longer than the other two rods because it extends all the way through the shoulder-vise parts. I used the same technique to mark the center points on the shoulder-vise parts.

I then face-glued the edgings and glued and clamped them to the front and back of the bench.

The space under the bench is put to use

Those big boxes in the base provide plenty of storage space. I placed eight drawers in the right-hand box. Plus, to take advantage of the space between the top of the box and the underside of the benchtop, I added a shallow through-drawer that extends from front to back, with a face on each end of the drawer, so it can be accessed from both sides of the workbench.

The left-hand box holds the parts of a project I'm building. The box includes a hinged shelf that pivots up and out of the way when it's not needed. The frame-and-panel doors keep dust from filling up the box.

Board jacks support long stock

The board jacks (one in front and one in back) are handy additions to the bench. When a board is clamped in the front or shoulder vise, the jack holds up the unsupported end. To accommodate boards of varying length, the jack is able to slide along the full length of the bench.

Power strips bring the juice

Because my bench is several feet from a wall, I added power strips along the front and back edges, making it easier to use power tools at the bench.

The bench has been serving me well for several years now. During that time, it has picked up plenty of scratches and dents, but it's as solid as ever. And I expect it's going to stay that way for many years to come.

Gluing thick veneer to a large surface

Large surfaces, like the top of my bench, are a challenge to veneer because it's difficult to get good clamping pressure over the entire surface. I have enough clamps for most jobs but nowhere near the number I'd need for my jumbo-size benchtop. And new clamps don't come cheap.

The answer proved to be a set of 10 shopmade clamping cauls. And because I was able to use mostly scrapwood, the total cost was less than I'd pay for a single commercial clamp.

It's easy to make these clamps. The top "jaw" is a 24-in. length of 4¾-in.-wide medium-density fiberboard (MDF) screwed to a 24-in.-long 2x3. The bottom jaw is a 24-in.-long 2x4. To prevent the MDF surfaces from ending up glued to the veneer, add a healthy coat of paste wax to each one. The ends of the jaws accept a 9-in.-long, ⅜-in.-dia. threaded rod that is fitted with a washer and nut on both ends.

To begin veneering, spread a generous coat of yellow glue on the mating surfaces of the veneer and particleboard. A short painter's roller allows you to spread the glue easily and quickly. When working with a large surface area, it's important to have a good assembly game-plan worked out because yellow glue can start to tack up in less than 10 minutes. You need to get the glue down and the clamps tightened up without delay.

Place the veneer glue-side down on the particleboard. Butt the pieces together, but don't add glue to the edges or worry about a perfect joint quite yet. Let the veneer overhang the particleboard all around.

Then start clamping down the veneer. To help avoid lengthwise buckling, tighten the clamps at one end and work toward the other.

Both the top and bottom surfaces of the particleboard must be veneered; if only the top is veneered, it can create uneven stresses that can cause the top to cup.

Once both sides have been veneered, true up the edge joints with a router equipped with a ⅜-in.-dia. straight bit. Use a long piece of stock as a straightedge and rout a ³⁄₁₆-in.-deep groove centered along the entire length of each joint line. Then use the clamping cauls to glue ⅜-in.-wide by ³⁄₁₆-in.-thick inlays into the grooves. This technique results in near-perfect edge joints.

Clamp the veneer to the particleboard with clamping cauls. No need to have a small fortune in clamps to do this glue-up. Shopmade clamping cauls get the job done for pennies.

Inlays conceal imperfect veneer joints. To clean up any gaps, a router and edge guide are used to cut a shallow groove centered on the long joint (top). Then add the inlay. Thin strips of cherry fill in the grooves, producing tight joint lines along the full length of the bench (above).

A Small Workbench That Works

PHIL LOWE

In the early 1970s, having completed my training in furniture-making, I found myself in need of a workbench. I figured I'd make one that would be large enough to hold all of my hand tools and small enough to move, guessing that it would be some time before I settled down. I wanted an all-purpose bench for planing, scraping, cutting joints, carving, and finishing. Cost was a concern because there was a slew of tools and machinery I wanted to buy, so I decided not to use any fancy or expensive hardwoods in its construction. For the original bench, I chose birch (sturdy and cheap) for the top and the frame, and I used construction-grade fir plywood for the side panels. That first version was a little on the low side, so I later corrected the problem by cutting down the original top and adding a new maple slab over it.

The relatively small size of the bench makes it comfortable to use. Unlike many larger benches, I can easily reach a workpiece resting on the top from all sides of the bench. It holds almost all of my hand tools—or at least the ones I use the most—keeping them well within reach. Also, this bench is small enough that it can be moved around the shop when needed. Loaded up with tools, it's heavy enough to stay in place while I'm using it. But I can break it down into manageable pieces, if need be, by removing the drawers and the top. I was particularly glad about this feature when I had to set it up in my first

Small but sturdy. This workbench is more than 40 years old, and it's still used daily for all facets of furniture-making.

apartment in a third-floor attic space where I worked for a while.

In the construction of the case, I used mortise-and-tenon joints with pins for all of the frame pieces, through- and blind-dovetails for the drawers, and housed dovetails for the drawer dividers. I built most of the frame with 8/4 birch, and I used 4/4 birch for the drawer dividers, the center partition, and the drawer fronts. I fashioned the side panels with ¾-in.-thick fir plywood, set into rabbets that were cut into the back edges of the legs and rails. Drawer runners—joined with tenons into mortises in the drawer dividers—are held to an inside frame by a screw in the back. The top is 8/4 maple, ripped to 3-in. widths that I glued together on edge for strength and stability.

To make the benchdog holes in the top, I cut a series of ¾-in. by ½-in. dadoes before laminating the top. I also cut the same size dadoes on every third board in a position that would line up with the dog on the vise, once it was fastened to the top. The overhang of the top is such that the dog holes are clear of the base so that they don't become clogged with sawdust. Also, I needed the overhang for clamping workpieces to the table. The overhang on the side above the drawers is smaller so that it doesn't restrict access to the tools in the top drawers. The new top is secured to the old original top (that I cut down to serve as a subtop) from underneath with lag screws, and that subtop is secured with lag screws through the top rails of the base cabinet.

This bench functions quite nicely. The vise will not only hold workpieces between its jaws, but it can also hold them between the dog on top of the vise and one placed into the benchtop. I sometimes set up workpieces, such as panels to be planed, so that they rest against a thinner batten that spans two dogs. With this setup I need to lift my plane on the return stroke to prevent the panel from sliding backward. And sometimes, when planing the ends or edges of panels or long boards, I use the vise to hold the workpiece and one of the drawers underneath to support it.

Looking back at the number of pieces I've built on this bench and remembering the number of workspaces it has inhabited, I realize how well it has served me all these many years. I'm sometimes asked how I could get by with such a relatively small top and without a tail vise. I have the additional work surface of a fold-down table near the bench that I use to lay out and organize parts of furniture I'm working on. And I honestly haven't felt the need for a tail vise, because dogs and a few clamps do the same job. I can proudly say that I have never driven a nail into the top to hold anything in place. There is one thing I would change if I were to make this bench again. The kick space between the bottom rail and the floor is too small, resulting in an occasional pain in my big toe. Also, someday I'd like to replace the fir plywood side panels with something a bit more attractive, but I don't imagine that will happen until my daughters finish school.

How it's used and what it holds

This benchtop's small size (32¼ in. by 59¼ in.) belies its versatility. The author's most-often-used hand tools fit compactly but comfortably in storage under the top. Layout tools, chisels, planes and spokeshaves, saws, rasps, files, scrapers, sanding blocks, hammers, and carving tools all have specific homes. There's even a spot for one very essential tool—a clipboard to record billable hours of time spent on jobs in the shop.

The vise is an adjustable clamp. A series of benchdog holes in the top line up with the center of the vise for clamping workpieces of varying lengths.

Securing the workpiece without clamps. A hardwood batten thinner than the workpiece butts against two benchdogs in the top to serve as a stop.

Out of harm's way. When it's not needed, this 3-ft. Starrett® straightedge lives in a slot under the benchtop.

Drawers do more than hold things. In combination with the vise, they also support workpieces such as this large mahogany carcase piece.

Every tool has its place. The contents of each drawer are custom-fit.

A New-Fangled Workbench

JOHN WHITE

For five years I worked as a cabinetmaker in a shop that used only hand tools for the simple reason that electricity wasn't available that far back in the woods. One lesson that I came away with was the importance of a good workbench—and lots of windows. I now work in a shop that is, if anything, over electrified, but a functional workbench is still important. Just because you're driving a car instead of a buggy doesn't mean you don't need a good road to get where you're going.

On a perfect bench, the various vises and stops would hold any size workpiece in the most convenient position for the job at hand. Traditional workbenches are adequate for clamping smaller pieces, a table leg or frame rail for instance, but most benches can't handle wide boards for edge- and face-planing or frame-and-panel assemblies.

Recently, I moved my shop and needed to build a new bench. I began by researching traditional American and European designs. I found that although our predecessors had many clever solutions to the problems of holding down a piece of wood, no one bench solved all or even most of the problems I had encountered in 25 years of woodworking. Frustrated, I finally decided to design a bench from the ground up.

At first I had no success. A design would address one problem but not another, or it would be far too complex. I was about to give up and build a traditional German bench when I came up with a design that incorporates pipe clamps into the bench's top, the front apron, and even the legs.

Planing beam slides on pipes

On the front of the bench is an adjustable, T-shaped planing beam that runs the full length of the bench. It is supported on both ends by the sliding tailpieces of Pony® pipe clamps. The ½-in. cast-iron pipes on which the clamps slide are incorporated into the bench's legs. I used Pony clamps throughout

Sliding height adjustment. Pipe-clamp tailpieces slide on cast-iron pipes held captive in the top and bottom of the bench. A T-shaped Douglas fir planing beam rides on the clamps.

Planing wedge. When used with the planing beam, long work is held against a wedge-shaped stop at the end of the bench. The harder you push against the work, the tighter it is held in place.

this project because they are well made and slide and lock very smoothly.

The planing beam continuously supports the full length of a board standing on edge. The stock for the planing beam can be as narrow as 2 in. and as wide as 30 in. The planing beam can be set to any position in seconds. Of all of the bench's features, the planing beam is the most useful. I use it dozens of times daily when building a piece of furniture.

You've probably noticed that there is no front vise to secure the board being planed. Instead, the force of the plane pushes the workpiece into a tapered planing wedge attached to the far left end of the bench. This is an ancient device, and for handplaning it is far more practical than any vise. You can flip the board end for end or turn the other edge up in an instant with one hand. You don't even have to put down your plane.

To make a shoulder vise when needed, I drilled holes 6 in. o.c. along the bench's front rail to mount pipe clamps horizontally. I pair up two clamps with a drop-in vise jaw, which

is just a length of 1¾-in. square hardwood. The jaw can be as short as 8 in. or longer than 6 ft. I have several jaws of different lengths.

The front vise can be used with the planing beam supporting the workpiece from below. This is useful because some procedures, such as chopping mortises, drive the work downward through the jaws of a conventional vise, scarring the wood.

Traditional tail vise is replaced with pipe clamps

On the bench's top, two pipe-clamp bars are recessed into a 10-in.-wide well, replacing a conventional tail vise and bench dogs. The clamp-tightening screws project from the right end of the bench, and the movable jaws project ¾ in. above the top. Both the fixed and movable jaws have oak faces. This clamp setup makes it easy to hold down boards for surface-planing because nothing projects above the board's surface to foul the tool. The top clamp bars have a clamping capacity of just over 7 ft.

Blocks of wood support the pipes. Each one is screwed to the frame of the bench with a drywall screw. The single screw allows each block to swing out of the way of the pipe-clamp tailpieces as they are slid to accommodate long work.

The top pipe clamps can also be used to hold panels in place that have other tools permanently attached, such as a vise or an electric grinder. I have a tilting drill-press vise attached to a square of medium-density

Horizontal clamps run full length. A pair of pipe clamps running under the benchtop hold work in the same way as a traditional tail vise.

Douglas fir workbench

To minimize costs, the author milled workbench stock from Douglas fir framing lumber, sawing clear sections from the center of 2×10s and 2×12s. The bench is fastened with drywall screws and lag bolts. Six pipe clamps in different configurations are used as vises.

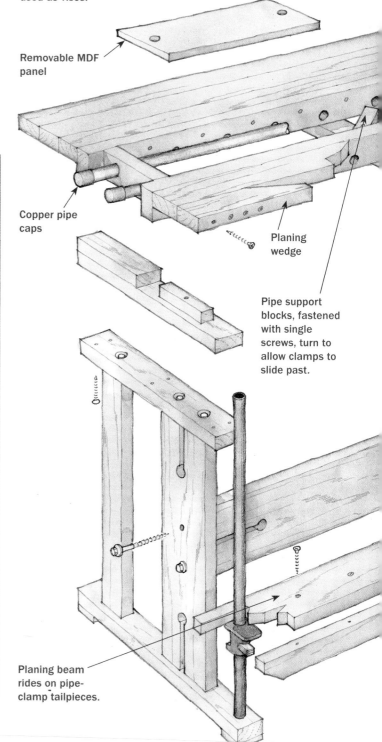

Removable MDF panel

Copper pipe caps

Planing wedge

Pipe support blocks, fastened with single screws, turn to allow clamps to slide past.

Planing beam rides on pipe-clamp tailpieces.

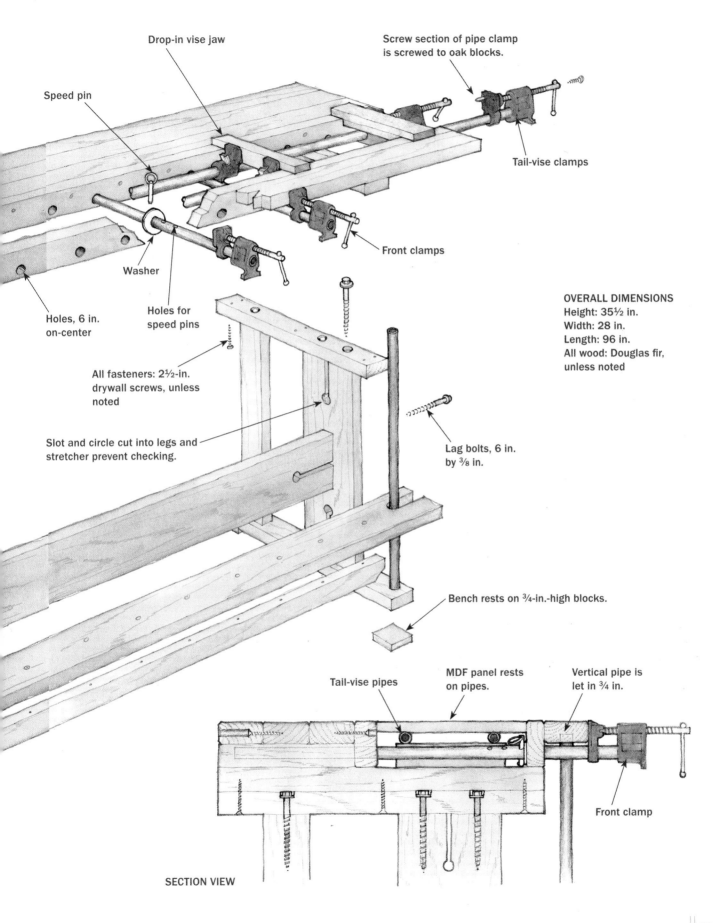

Drop-in vise jaw

Screw section of pipe clamp
is screwed to oak blocks.

Speed pin

Tail-vise clamps

Washer

Front clamps

Holes, 6 in.
on-center

Holes for
speed pins

OVERALL DIMENSIONS
Height: 35½ in.
Width: 28 in.
Length: 96 in.
All wood: Douglas fir,
unless noted

All fasteners: 2½-in.
drywall screws, unless
noted

Slot and circle cut into legs and
stretcher prevent checking.

Lag bolts, 6 in.
by ⅜ in.

Bench rests on ¾-in.-high blocks.

Tail-vise pipes

MDF panel rests
on pipes.

Vertical pipe is
let in ¾ in.

Front clamp

SECTION VIEW

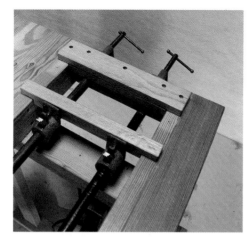

Oak blocks span tail-vise clamps. The screw ends of the pipe clamps are screwed to the end of the bench through holes drilled in the clamp faces.

Pipes rest on blocks that turn. Tail-vise pipe clamps are supported by blocks fastened with one screw. To slide a clamp past, turn the block.

Front clamps are easy to adjust. The clamps fit in holes in the bench front and are secured with large washers and speed pins.

fiberboard (MDF) that I clamp to the bench for metalworking or for holding a piece of wood to be carved. I plan to design a drop-in router table for the bench; there's enough space between the pipe-clamp bars to fit a small machine.

When the top clamps aren't in use, the well is covered by several sections of ¾-in. MDF that simply drop in and lay on top of the pipes. Because MDF is so inexpensive, I treat the panels as sacrificial surfaces. I cut into them, screw jigs to them, whack them with a hammer, and when they get too chewed up, I toss them. To save my back, I buy precut MDF meant for shelving; it comes either 12 in. or 16 in. wide. This precut stock is useful for all manner of jigs and prototypes, and I always have a few lengths around the shop.

Douglas fir makes a solid bench

The bench, as I built it, is 8 ft. long and was designed to accommodate fairly large work, such as doors and other architectural millwork. The design can be shortened or lengthened, and it could be reversed end for end if you are left-handed.

I built the bench out of Douglas fir instead of hardwood. Douglas fir at its best is a dense, stable wood that machines cleanly and holds fasteners well, important attributes given the way I wanted to assemble the bench.

Wide planks—2×10s and 2×12s—of Douglas fir framing lumber will often be sawn right out of the center of the log, and a half or more of the board will be quartersawn and knot free, with tight, straight grain. By carefully choosing and ripping these planks, you can get some beautiful material for a lot less than the price of even mediocre furniture woods. Some of the trimmed-out wood that isn't good enough for the bench can still be used for other projects, such as shelves or sawhorses.

If you start with green lumber, sticker it for a few months to get the moisture content down. To prevent checking, trim the ends to get a clean surface and then apply duct tape over the end grain. Even if you start with kiln-dried wood, give it a couple of weeks indoors to stabilize before starting to cut. Use the best wood for the frame, benchtop, and beam, saving lesser quality stock for the leg assembly.

Screw joinery is fast and strong

My method of assembling the bench with drywall screws and lag screws (and no fitted-and-glued joinery) is unconventional, but I've used this style of construction for years. The finished bench is rock solid, and the joinery goes quickly.

Most of the screws were counterbored with a ⅜-in. drill, sometimes quite deeply, to bring the screw heads ¾ in. shy of the edge being joined. On the 3-in.-wide, edge-jointed benchtop boards, the counterbore is 2¼ in. deep. The deep bore minimizes the amount of wood under the screw head, which in turn minimizes the loosening of the joint as the stock shrinks.

After drilling the counterbore, follow up with a long bit to drill a clearance hole for the screw shank. Then line up the pieces to be joined and install the screws a couple of turns to mark the centers, drill pilot holes at the marks in the adjoining piece, and assemble the bench.

One of the advantages of this type of construction is that if the wood shrinks and the joints loosen up, you can retighten everything in a few minutes with a screwdriver. I did this about a month after assembling the bench, and it has stayed solid ever since. Don't overtighten the screws. Excessively crushing the wood under the screw's head ruins the resilience that allows a joint to flex slightly and remain tight.

Lift-out MDF panels. The panels, cut in different lengths from MDF scraps, make a durable yet disposable center surface for the bench. The panels get removed when the tail-vise pipe clamps are in use.

The keyhole slots in the legs and stretcher are functional; as the boards shrink, they allow the wood to flex without cracking. In effect, they are preemptive cracks that look a lot better than the ones that would form randomly otherwise. When you install the lag bolts, drill clearance and pilot holes and go easy on the torque when you tighten them up. The joint will be stronger if you don't over-stress the threads in the stretcher's end grain.

The pipes used with the clamps cut easily with a hacksaw or a small pipe cutter. For the smoothest operation of the clamps, clean up any burrs along the length of each pipe with a file and then smooth it down with emery paper. This is a messy operation, creating a staining black dust, so do it away from your woodworking area. Wipe down each pipe with a rag and paint thinner when you are done.

Holding Your Work

GARRETT HACK

A good workbench is one of the most important tools in any shop. It doesn't need to be fancy or have vises to be useful, just a nice, flat work surface and a base sturdy and heavy enough to stay put. The challenge then becomes how to hold your work securely and easily, so you can concentrate your energy on controlling your tools, not on work slipping around.

Furniture parts come in a huge variety of sizes and shapes. Take, for example, a chair. To plane the straight seat rails, you must hold them flat on a bench. To shoot their edges you need to support them upright. To shape back legs that are curved, you need a different solution, as you might for carving the crest rail or for holding any of these parts when chopping mortises.

Fortunately, for every kind of holding problem, there are at least a few solutions: stops, holdfasts, bench hooks, miter blocks, clamps, and more. The best are quick, positive, and easily put to work.

Stops are quick and simple

In an average day, I plane all sorts of parts held flat on my bench. Some are narrow, some wide, some long, and some short. By far the simplest way to hold them (and plenty of other pieces that aren't flat) is to use a single, solid stop of some kind.

I use wood stops because they are easy to make and to customize for holding an odd-shaped part, and they won't damage my tools

if I run into one. The stop I use most often is a simple hardwood benchdog dropped into one of the holes on my benchtop. Although this gives me flexibility in positioning a workpiece anywhere along the bench, a fixed stop either mortised into the benchtop or securely screwed to it can be just as useful in the same situations.

It's ideal to be able to adjust the height of your benchdog just barely above the surface

Benchdogs make great stops. Made of ash, oak or similar hardwood, benchdogs are easy to make and replace, as necessary. A wood spring helps hold it in place.

Planing against a single point. The easiest way to hold a board when planing is to use a single benchdog.

Use two points of pressure with wide stock. Multiple stops help keep wider stock from moving sideways during planing.

for planing thin drawer sides or sticking out a few inches for larger work. If you mortise a benchdog into your bench, fit it snugly so that it requires only a tap to move it up or down. Because I am often moving my benchdogs (I use them in pairs with my tail vise), I've fitted them with ash springs that keep them in their holes. Lee Valley® makes similar brass dogs that drop into round holes easily drilled into a bench.

I can make a new wooden stop to fit almost any need, such as cutting a V-groove into the face to hold parts with mitered ends. I have a dog with a brad in the face that pricks into small pieces to hold them better. But a stop with a nice, square face is still the most useful, and a little planing dresses it up when it gets worn.

There are times when a single stop does not provide enough support, such as when planing wide stock aggressively. In this case I use a benchdog and clamp an additional stop to my bench to prevent sideways movement (see the top right photo). Or I clamp a board across the entire end to work against.

Versatile V-cut blocks. To chamfer or put a lamb's tongue on a square leg, make two blocks with deep V-cuts and place them against a benchdog. The blocks hold the legs in the best position for working the corners with a chisel.

Three dogs. Adding pins or V-grooves to your dogs helps them hold thin or mitered stock.

Planing thin, straight stock. This jig is simply a piece of plywood with thin, perpendicular fences. Butt the jig against a benchdog to hold it in place.

Stops for thin work

To plane thin stock, I set up a jig that's simply a flat piece of plywood with thin pieces of wood tacked down to it. One piece of wood acts as a stop; the other piece acts as a fence (see the photo at left). The whole assembly is butted against a benchdog on my bench.

To plane a piece that is curved and very thin, one of my favorite solutions is to tack a small brass escutcheon pin on a flat board and butt the piece against it. It's best to use brass because it's a soft metal and will cause less damage to your plane blade should you hit the pin.

Bird's-mouth stops

Planing a board on edge is a common-enough task that it's worth making either of two simple wooden jigs to hold the board

Planing thin, curved stock. A brass escutcheon pin tacked into a flat board (left) serves as a ministop for smaller workpieces (above). Because brass is soft, it won't damage your tools if you run into it.

securely on your benchtop. One is a thick board with a bird's mouth cut into the end that is clamped to the bench. It works easily, not only as a stop, but also as some vertical support. A slightly more elaborate version has a wedge to lock the part in place (see the photos at right).

To plane a short apron I butt the piece against a bird's-mouth stop and use a hand alongside the plane to steady both the apron and the plane. This technique is simple, quick, and, with practice, not difficult. Where I want a little more support, say, for a thin board, I clamp the end away from the stop in a wood hand screw laid flat on the bench. I've held longer boards in two or three such hand screws. Merely clamping a board upright with bar clamps also works for a task such as cutting a mortise, but when planing they get in the way.

Stops for curved work

Much of the furniture I build has a lot of curved parts. Some of the curves are shallow enough that I can hold the part on the bench as I would a flat piece. When shooting edges, for example, I butt the workpiece against a stop and work carefully to keep the piece balanced and steady.

For more shapely parts that don't balance easily against a stop—the curved apron of a demilune table, for example—I still use a stop but with one or more support boards clamped to my bench. These outriggers, as I like to call them, are scraps about 2 in. wide clamped in such a way that they provide sideways support at two or more points.

Locking the workpiece in the bird's-mouth. A bird's-mouth stop holds a board on edge and allows you to plane, sand, or carve the edge safely without the use of a vise. A bird's-mouth holds stock remarkably steady, but a wedge (above) offers extra stability and a quick release.

Edge-planing curved work. Butt the end of the stock into a bird's-mouth and the middle against a benchdog. Steady the work with your left hand.

Holdfasts: One smack, and the work is secured. The shaft of a holdfast wedges into a hole in the workbench. Be sure your benchtop is at least 2 in. thick or the holdfast may split the top.

Odd shapes are no problem. A holdfast and a stop are all that's needed to hold this burl because it has a flat bottom. If your work doesn't have a flat bottom, use wedges to level the piece.

Holdfasts provide a quick, tight hold

Ancient Roman benches had no holding aids besides a simple stop and iron holdfast. A holdfast is simply an upside-down L-shaped bar that wedges into a hole in the bench with a slight rap on the top. Rap a few more times for firmer downward pressure, or from behind to loosen it. Holdfasts are useful for holding work of almost any shape flat on the bench (flattening out any bow as well). They can also be driven into holes in the front of a bench for holding long boards and wide panels upright, as if they were in a vise.

A holdfast offers quick and secure clamping pressure. The more you drive the holdfast into the hole in the bench, the more tightly it wedges in, providing more clamping pressure. A light rap from behind with a wooden mallet quickly releases the clamping pressure.

With a model that has a screw on top, insert the holdfast into its hole, place it on the work, and tighten the screw until snug.

A holdfast may come loose if lateral pressure is placed on the workpiece. Often, using a holdfast together with a benchdog is one of the fastest ways to hold your work and keep it in place. I try to use the holdfast to steady the work and then work against the dog.

Installing a traditional holdfast is fairly straightforward: It requires one or more holes in your bench ¹⁄₁₆ in. larger than the diameter of the shaft. The problem is where to drill the holes without turning your bench into Swiss cheese—and getting past the emotional hurdle of actually drilling those holes. I suggest at least three evenly spaced holes 14 in. to 18 in. from the front of the bench.

Holdfasts: What's out there

Most of the traditional holdfasts come in two sizes: 5 in. and 8 in. The smaller models can hold stock up to 1 in. thick. Choose a larger model for use with thicker or irregular stock.

Newer holdfasts incorporate a screw at the top of the arm. These holdfasts are not hit with a mallet. By tightening the screw, the shaft wedges within a hole drilled into a benchtop. Veritas has a model similar to the classic Record, and the shaft has scalelike rings on it that hold it in the hole. The Record holdfast relies on a collar mortised into the bench.

Jorgensen® has a plastic holdfast that is essentially a large plastic screw with an arm. It has a hefty plastic nut that goes under the bench and requires you to reach under your bench to release it. Its arm reach is about 3 in., but the plastic will save the edges of your chisels and gouges.

Beware of holdfasts made from cast iron, because the shafts are brittle and can crack and break when placed under stress. The material of a holdfast should have some flex to it. Some of the cast-iron varieties are being redesigned with a steel shank. Most of these holdfasts are made in Taiwan, and although they're pretty rough looking, they will do the job. Woodcraft now sells a U.S. version made with ductile iron, which is less brittle than cast steel.

—Timothy Sams

Five holdfasts on the market. Pictured from left to right: Jorgensen Quick Release Hold Down; 5-in. and 8-in. traditional holdfasts; Veritas Hold-Down; Gross Stabil® Bench Clamping Set.

Clamps are versatile mechanisms

I use both light-duty bar clamps and heavier ones with a jaw reach of about 5 in. Unless the piece is small, two clamps always hold more securely than one; both hold the piece in place and work together to prevent slippage from side to side. The problem is that the clamps are typically placed somewhere along the front edge of the bench, where they get in the way.

Nevertheless, clamps can be the best method to hold work on top of the bench: irregular shapes, large work such as big tabletops, or jigs for working specially shaped pieces. By placing the clamps along the sides or back of my bench, I get them out of the way of my prime work surface along the front edge. I try to make jigs large enough to get the clamps well out of the way. Clamps also have better holding power if spread far apart. Whenever possible, I try to use a benchdog

Wood hand screw holds long boards on edge. For longer, more unwieldy stock, use a hand screw clamped to the bench.

Holding turned legs with a bar clamp. Glue small blocks with protruding nails onto the jaws of the clamp. Secure the clamp in a vice.

Tenon shaping on curved work. Use two wedges plus a clamp to keep the piece in place. If the larger block wants to move, place a benchdog behind it.

as a stop somewhere along the bench and eliminate one of the clamps.

For larger pieces that don't fit on top of the bench so comfortably, I regularly clamp these upright along the front edge of my bench, with bar clamps going across the bench, if necessary.

When chopping tenon shoulders on a curved apron, I place a block underneath to add stability under the workpiece and to break up the fibers I am chopping. I butt one end against a stop and use a single clamp to hold everything in place.

Legs, carvings, and irregular work

Table and chair legs can be difficult to hold flat on the bench. A workable method is to first clamp the leg lengthwise between the jaws of a bar clamp and then clamp the assembly to the top of the bench with wooden hand screws.

You can also chamfer the edges on a square, tapered leg by securing it to the bench with V-blocks and a benchdog. I don't see a particular need to clamp the piece to these blocks, but if it becomes unstable while working on it, I do.

Clamping odd-shaped stock requires a good bit of creativity. There are products that may help, but for the most part they work on the principle of wedging the piece between two or three points to keep it stable. I try to use benchdogs and either a clamp or a hold-fast just because they are the most efficient for me. Don't be afraid to experiment, but there is no reason to make it too complicated.

Bench hook: An ancient device that still works. A bench hook holds the work steady for both cutting with a push saw and shooting the end of a board with a handplane.

Use a miter block with thin stock. Held in a vise it allows smaller stock to be held securely for cutting.

How a bench hook works

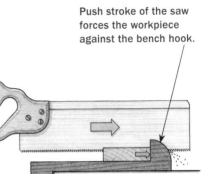

Push stroke of the saw forces the workpiece against the bench hook.

Edge of the bench acts as a stop for the bench hook.

Bench hooks and miter blocks can secure small stock

I use bench hooks and miter blocks when stock is too small to clamp or hold against a benchdog.

A bench hook is an ancient device: a flat board with blocks on opposite sides. One block locks over the edge of the bench; the other holds the workpiece. The bench hook is good for holding small stock for making repeated sawcuts or for planing the end of a board. Used to shoot end grain, a bench hook not only supports the board but also backs up the fibers at the end of the cut, preventing them from tearing out. Pairs of bench hooks of various sizes are useful for holding long boards or wide panels flat on the bench.

For even smaller stock, I use a small miter block—a 1½-in.-thick block of wood with a rabbet cut into it. Held in the vise, this block can make it easier to cut delicate inlay work, veneer or other small strips of wood. I cut 90-degree and 45-degree angles (and other angles) into the block to guide my saw. For a backsaw I place the block in the vise with the rabbet facing me. For a pull saw I orient the rabbet away from me.

A bench, no matter how complex, is only as useful as you make it. I respect my bench, but it's not precious. For common, everyday holding problems drill a few holes in your bench if need be, and set yourself up with a dog, clamps, holdfasts, or whatever. A simple, secure holddown lets you concentrate all of your efforts on controlling your tools, allowing you to do better, safer, more enjoyable work.

Making Sense of Vises

GARRETT HACK

Hold work vertically for sawing dovetails or planing end grain. A scrap piece of similar thickness, clamped in the opposite side of the front vise, prevents the vise from racking.

A good bench vise is nearly as useful as a shop apprentice. On my bench I have a front vise and a large tail vise—I call them my right- and left-hand men. It's hard to imagine woodworking without them; they hold my work firmly so that I can concentrate fully on powering and controlling the tool I'm using.

In general, you'll find vises at two locations on a woodworker's bench: one on the long side of the bench, typically at the left-hand corner for right-handed woodworkers, and another on the short side at the opposite end.

The first, known variously as a side vise or front vise, matches the mental picture that most people have of a vise, with a movable jaw capturing work between it and the edge of the bench.

The second, c
can clamp work
often used to ho
pinched betweer
and another in o
the benchtop. To
meet all of a woo(
when it comes to l
within reach.

A front vise
vertically or

A front vise, typica
left-front corner, is i
clamp a board to pl
leg while shaping it,

Typical workbench vises

END VISE
Usually found at the end of the bench, opposite the front vise, it is used with benchdogs to hold work flat for tasks like surface planing or chopping mortises.

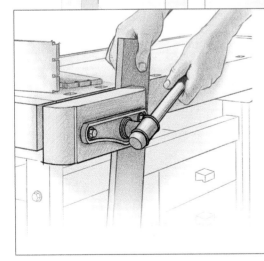

FRONT VISE
It typically occupies the left-front corner of the bench and is used to hold stock upright for sawing or for working edges.

Secure long boards on edge. A block clamped in the tail vise supports the opposite end.

Steady a wide panel. A sawhorse provides support underneath, with the opposite end clamped to the bench apron.

for sawing dovetails. The most common design is quite simple: a jaw of wood, or cast iron lined with wood, that moves with a single screw and a T-handle. The rest of the vise is mortised into the front edge of the bench. Mine opens about 10 in. and has about 4 in. of depth.

Many of the front vises on the market are fairly easy to fit to a benchtop. Look for one that has a large screw with well-cut Acme threads. These are the same square threads found on good clamps; they can smoothly deliver lots of force over a long life.

To hold long boards, wide panels, or doors securely on edge in a front vise, you need the added support of the deep front apron of the

Hold wide workpieces on edge. The vise screw prevents a wide piece from going all the way through the vise (left). A clamp seated in a dog hole provides extra support (right).

bench. Properly installed, the fixed half of the vise should be mortised into the bench so that the movable jaw clamps against the apron. This creates a great deal of stability, making it possible to clamp most boards on edge with no other support. For very long boards, just put one end in the front vise and rest the other on a short board clamped in the tail or end vise, much like a board jack on traditional benches. You can clamp a large tabletop vertically against the front edge of a bench, one end held in the front vise and the other held by a bar clamp across the bench.

A problem can arise, though, when clamping on just one side of the vise, such as when holding just the end of a much larger piece,

clamping pieces vertically for laying out or sawing dovetails, or holding tapered or oddly shaped pieces. When one side of the jaw is applying all the pressure—or trying to—it is very hard on the screw and any alignment rods, and can even distort them. One solution is to slip a block as thick as the workpiece into the other side of the jaw (use a wedge for odd shapes). This keeps the jaws parallel so you can apply all the pressure you need. Some bench manufacturers equip their front vises with a threaded stop that does the same job.

Types of front vises

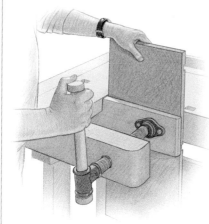

ARM VISE
An arm vise works well on wide boards. There are no screws or rods in the way. But the right-angled arm limits clamping force, which reduces the ability to clamp long boards horizontally.

Build it yourself. Many companies sell the hardware for arm vises. Look for a large screw with square-cut threads.

CAST IRON
The most popular front vise is cast iron. A steel rod or two keep the jaw aligned. Some also have a quick-action release for faster jaw adjustments.

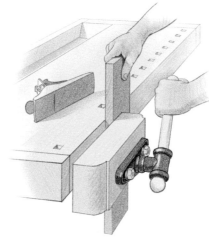

WOODEN-JAWED
A wooden-jawed vise operates like its cast-iron cousin. The movable jaw is typically made from the same material as the bench. Some models offer quick-release.

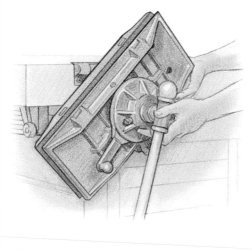

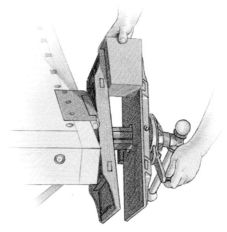

PATTERNMAKER'S VISE
A patternmaker's vise can hold oddly shaped work at any angle. The vise body can pivot up and over the bench until the jaws are parallel to the benchtop. The jaws also can rotate 360 degrees and angle toward each other for holding tapered work.

A vise that holds work flat

At the other end of the bench, you typically will find one of two distinct types of vises, known as end vises or tail vises. Their main purpose is to hold work flat on the surface of the bench.

A traditional tail vise, with one row of dog holes along the front edge of the bench and several more in the movable jaw, allows you to hold work flat over nearly the entire length of the bench. This is ideal for holding long boards to smooth a face, bead one edge, or hold a leg while chopping a mortise. You can also clamp across the grain to bevel a panel end or shape the skirt of a chest side. Be careful to apply only modest pressure to hold the work, or you will bow it up.

The tail vise is also great for holding long or odd pieces at any angle: There are no

An end vise holds work flat. Aligned with a row of dog holes, this vise has a wide capacity. It can hold smaller work and pieces nearly as large as the benchtop. It's ideal for smoothing a tabletop.

A secure grip for cross-grain work. The end vise allows you to clamp a panel across its width for tasks such as planing a bevel on the end.

An end vise also handles awkward shapes. Pieces like this curved table apron can be held securely for scraping or other tasks.

For chopping, a spacer keeps the work off the vise jaw. The pounding could damage the vise. The best support is on the benchtop itself, right over a leg.

screws in the way and the hefty construction tends to prevent racking on odd shapes. Also, it can hold a workpiece at right angles to the bench edge, ideal for planing an end-grain edge, shooting a miter on a molding, or paring a tenon shoulder.

One drawback with this vise is that the large movable jaw can sag. A misaligned jaw makes it difficult to hold work flat on the benchtop. Avoid chopping or pounding over the movable jaw; it isn't as solid as the benchtop itself. Support the work as much as possible over the bench, with the least amount of jaw open. I keep small, square blocks handy to shim my work toward the bench or protect it from the dogs. I shouldn't have to say this, but never sit on your tail vise.

Another type of end vise

The other popular type of end vise looks and works like a front vise, except that the movable jaw is mounted to, and set parallel with, the end of the bench. If I had to outfit a bench with just one vise, it would be this type (see the top right drawing on the facing page). My small traveling bench has an old front vise mounted on one end in line with a row of dog holes.

Some end vises of this type have a jaw that spans the entire width of the bench. Equipped with a dog on each end of the jaw, and paired with a double row of dog holes down the front and back of the bench, this is a great system for holding wide parts flat on the benchtop. Several ready-made benches are built this way. Lee Valley also sells the necessary hardware for making the vise yourself.

Types of end vises

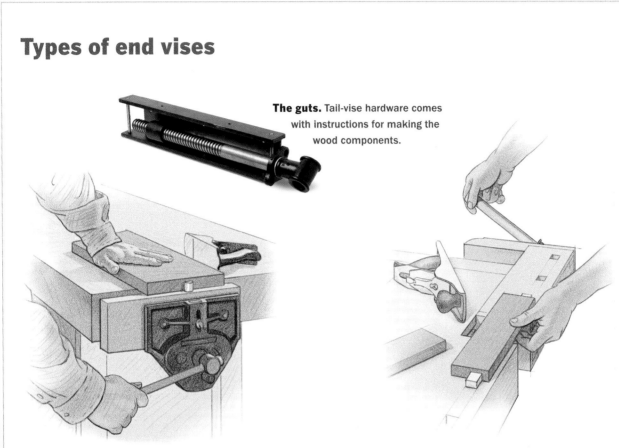

The guts. Tail-vise hardware comes with instructions for making the wood components.

CAST IRON

Same vise, different location. The cast-iron front vise also works well as an end vise—a smart solution if you have room or money for only one vise.

TAIL VISE

The traditional end vise. The movable jaw is a thick section of the bench's front edge, about 18 in. long. Dog holes hold work flat on the surface. The jaws also can hold work at an angle.

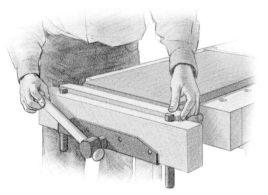

FULL WIDTH

A modern variation spans the width of the bench. With two rows of dog holes, the wide jaw of this vise is ideal for holding wider panels.

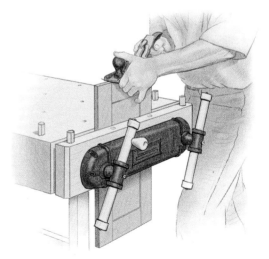

TWIN-SCREW

A twin-screw model can clamp wide stock vertically. A chain connects the two screws to prevent racking.

Thirteen Bench Vises

MATT KENNEY

My woodworking improved dramatically after I installed a vise on my bench. With a vise to hold my work, I could mark and cut accurate dovetails, plane square edges, and rout profiles without the board sliding all over.

That's why I'm convinced that a bench vise is as important as any tool in the shop. Whether you use power tools, hand tools, or both, a good bench vise will help you work more accurately, efficiently, and safely.

A bench vise is meant to hold your work securely. A good vise not only does that well, but also opens and closes easily, has jaws that clamp squarely to the stock and hold it tight, and is versatile enough to handle a variety of woodworking tasks. A bad vise doesn't hold boards tight, or has a nut that pops off the threads when you tighten the jaws.

There are two basic choices. Cast-iron vises (left) can be used right out of the box and give you the option of adding wooden jaws. With vise hardware (right), you'll need to make and install wooden jaws.

Narrowing the field

It wouldn't be practical to test every vise available, so I focused on front vises, because they are the first serious vise woodworkers buy and can be the only type they'll need. Front vises are not difficult to install and they can be used as end vises. All have a screw between two guide bars, but there are two types. You can buy a fully assembled cast-iron vise, which includes metal jaws, or simply the vise hardware, which supplies the screw and guide bars. You supply the wooden jaws.

Both types have their advantages. Vise hardware is less obtrusive, because there is less visible metal and the jaws can be made to match your benchtop. Cast-iron vises are easier to install and most have a built-in benchdog.

When I had the option, I chose quick-release models, because slowly winding a vise open to plane a drawer or use the built-in bench dogs isn't efficient or fun.

We also tested two twin-screw vises. One model was discontinued, so we're publishing only the results for the Veritas model. Like the other vises, it can be used as either a front vise or an end vise. Though it doesn't have the quick-release feature, it can clamp stock

Quick release is faster. On trigger-release vises (top), a lever near the handle drops the nut so the outer jaw slides quickly to where you need it. This style is based on the iconic vises by Record. On some quick-release vises, a quarter turn releases the nut (above).

Dogs add versatility. Most cast-iron vises have a benchdog built into the front jaw (top). With vise hardware (above), you add a dog hole (or two) to the wooden front jaw.

for a semester on tasks such as dovetailing, planing, carving, and working on shaped parts. Fitzgerald and I also did our own testing, and weighed in on the results.

Note that the vises were used heavily for hand-tool work, which puts the most stress on a vise. Any vise that stands up to sawing and planing should be fine for machine work like routing and drilling. The students benefited, too. These vises were a big improvement over the old ones in their shop. And every vise was donated to the school by the manufacturer or supplier.

The makings of a good vise

We don't ask vises to do much, but there are features to look for other than the ability to clamp wood securely. There's an easy fix for vises that rack (see the photos on the facing page), but the less you have to deal with racking the better. We checked for racking by clamping a board vertically on one side of the vise and measuring how far out of parallel the jaws were on the other side.

Also, check the vertical alignment. The jaws should clamp squarely to the stock from top to bottom. Because the screw is at the bottom of the vise, the bottom tends to pull in as pressure is applied. To compensate, the moving jaw on cast-iron vises should be canted in slightly at the top. (With vise hardware, taper the front jaw so it's slightly thicker at the top.)

There are two types of quick release: trigger and twist. I recommend a twist-release vise, because the nut disengages when the screw is turned. This makes it easy to hold a workpiece in one hand and use the other to turn the screw and adjust the front jaw. On a trigger-release vise, you must pull and hold a trigger to disengage the nut. It can be tricky to do this while moving the jaw with the same hand.

vertically in the center of its jaws, making it easier to dovetail wide boards. That's a compelling benefit.

To put these vises to the test, each one had to be used daily for a variety of tasks, and they had to be compared side by side. I needed help and found it in the School of Art + Design at Purchase College in New York. Dennis Fitzgerald, who oversees the woodshop there, installed the vises in the shop, and the students used and abused them

No fix needed. Kenney was surprised to find that some vises racked very little. He could tighten the jaws enough to hold a board for dovetailing and not have the board shift at all (left). On the Veritas vise, you can place a wide board between the two screws (below), and the vise applies clamping pressure equally.

Easy fix. Some vise jaws pivot and lose their grip when a piece must be clamped in only one side of the vise. The solution is to clamp a scrap of the same thickness at the other end.

With a quick-release vise, an important feature is how well the nut engages. If the nut pops or jumps when you tighten the screw, the vise doesn't tighten and your workpiece can fall out. Finally, check the fit and finish. Rough castings can scratch or cut your fingers or workpiece, and screws that don't turn smoothly are frustrating.

And the winners are...

Among the cast-iron vises, the Jorgensen is the best. Its twist-release mechanism works very well, and it has a big metal benchdog that moves smoothly and stays in place. The vertical alignment was always dead-on under pressure, and it racked the second least. The best value is the Groz rapid-action vise. It performed very well, and I like the action of the twist release.

Among vise hardware, the Veritas twin-screw is easily the best. It has the biggest clamping capacity and doesn't rack. The front jaw can be skewed for tapered parts or to overcome racking force if you clamp something outside the screws. The Veritas doesn't have quick release, but everything else about it is so nice we didn't miss it. We picked the large quick-release front vise sold by Lee Valley as the best value. It's a solid performer at a good price.

Anant® 52½ ED

Groz 9-in. Rapid Action

Jet 9½-in. Quick Release

Jorgensen Rapid-Acting
Bench Vise

Medium Quick-Release Steel
Bench Vise (Lee Valley)

Rockler® 9-in. Quick
Release Workbench Vise

Shop Fox® Quick Release
Wood Vise

Wilton® 79A Pivot
Jaw Woodworkers
Vise-Rapid Acting

Cast-iron vises

VISE NAME	SUPPLIER (PRODUCT NUMBER)	
Anant 52½ ED	www.highlandwoodworking.com (199302)	
Groz 9-in. Rapid Action	www.woodcraft.com (148437)	
Jet 9½-in. Quick Release	www.southern-tool.com (WMH708569)	
Jorgensen Rapid-Acting Bench Vise	www.woodcraft.com (16T52)	
Medium Quick-Release Steel Bench Vise	www.leevalley.com (10G04.12)	
Rockler 9-in. Quick Release Workbench Vise	www.rockler.com (33487)	
Shop Fox 9-in. Quick-Release Wood Vise	www.japanwoodworker.com (66.252.5)	
Wilton 79A Pivot Jaw Woodworkers Vise-Rapid Acting	www.southern-tool.com (WMH63218)	

Vise hardware

VISE NAME	SUPPLIER (PRODUCT NUMBER)	
Economy Quick-Release Front Vise	www.woodcraft.com (145444)	
Large Quick-Release Front Vise	www.leevalley.com (Large, 70G08.10)	
Quick-Release Front Vise	www.woodcraft.com (17A11)	
Rockler Quick-Release End Vise	www.rockler.com (37180)	
Veritas Twin-Screw Vise	www.leevalley.com (05G12.21)	

Economy Quick-Release
Front Vise (Woodcraft)

Large Quick-Release Front Vise
(Lee Valley)

STREET PRICE	QUICK RELEASE	JAW WIDTH	OPENING CAPACITY	EASE OF USE	RACKING	VERTICAL ALIGNMENT	COMMENTS
$$	Yes, lever	9 in.	12¾ in.	Poor	0.05	Good	Quick-release nut doesn't re-engage well.
$	Yes, twist	9 in.	13 in.	Excellent	0.09	Excellent	Must add wooden front jaw to get a benchdog.
$$	Yes, lever	9½ in.	9½ in.	Good	0.06	Excellent	Release lever is not easy to operate.
$$	Yes, twist	10 in.	12 in.	Excellent	0.04	Excellent	Steel benchdog moves easily and stays in place once set.
$$	Yes, twist	9 in.	13 in.	Good	0.13	Good	Doesn't open and close smoothly.
$$	Yes, twist	9 in.	13 in.	Good	0.08	Excellent	Doesn't open and close smoothly.
$	Yes, lever	9 in.	10¼ in.	Good	0.08	Excellent	Paint chipped easily.
$$$	Yes, twist	10 in.	13 in.	Good	0.06	Very good	Quick-release nut doesn't re-engage immediately.

STREET PRICE	QUICK RELEASE	OPENING CAPACITY	EASE OF USE	RACKING	COMMENTS
$	Yes, twist	11 ½ in.	Fair	0.15	Too much play in screw and guide bars caused jaw to open and close poorly.
$$	Yes, twist	13 in.	Good	0.09	Nut occasionally fails to disengage when you twist screw to pull jaw out.
$$$	Yes, twist	14¼ in.	Good	0.05	Required more force to open and close jaw than other vises.
$$	Yes, twist	13 in.	Good	0.06	Can clamp up to 6-in.-wide boards between guide post and screw.
$$$	No	12 in.	Excellent	N/A	Can clamp up to 16-in.-wide boards between screws; two handles are a nuisance at times.

Quick-Release Front Vise
(Woodcraft)

Rockler Quick-Release
End Vise

Veritas Twin-Screw Vise

Installing vises

CAST IRON

Just bolt and go. If necessary, install a spacer under the benchtop to keep the top of the jaws just below the top of the bench.

Get more with a long jaw. Mortising a long wooden jaw over the rear jaw makes it easier to clamp wide and long boards.

VISE HARDWARE

Start with the baseplate. The first step is to screw the baseplate to the bottom of the benchtop. Then clamp the rear jaw in place and mark the holes for the screw and guide bars.

Attach the rear jaw. After you've drilled holes for the screw and guide bars, bolt the rear jaw to the benchtop. Barrel nuts mortised in from the bottom of the benchtop capture the bolts.

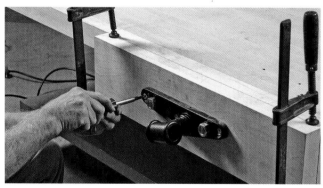

Bolt the front jaw in place. Clamp the wooden front jaw to the rear jaw, and then install the screw plate and guide bars.

VERITAS TWIN-SCREW VISE

As the screws turn. Clamp the front jaw in place and start cranking the screws. When tight, attach the screw plates.

Attach the nuts. The round nuts fit into holes drilled into the rear jaw, and the square bases are screwed in place. Then attach the jaw to the benchtop.

Clip the chain in. A small spring clip holds the ends of the chain together. The chain turns a sprocket on each screw, and lets you open and close both screws with one hand.

Expand Your Workbench with Versatile Bench Hooks

CHRIS GOCHNOUR

Even in a contemporary workshop filled with power tools and timesaving devices, it often is more practical and convenient to perform some woodworking tasks, such as final fitting of joinery and detail work, at the workbench using hand tools.

Since temporarily relocating with my family to a two-bedroom apartment in downtown Washington, D.C., I've embraced this notion to the extreme. My shop here, tucked into the corner of one of the bedrooms, consists of my bench and my most essential hand tools. Just as important is a collection of bench hooks that I draw on regularly, which are capable of performing a range of tasks, including cutting square and mitered ends as well as fine-tuning miters and ends to perfection. Even in less extreme shop conditions than mine, these bench hooks are indispensable tools.

Beyond the basic bench hook

In its simplest form, the bench hook is a platform that can be held steady against a workbench for performing tasks such as crosscutting and handplaning. A hook on the underside of the platform fits over the edge of the bench and keeps the platform steady as forward pressure is applied. A stop block on top of the platform, perpendicular to the edge of the bench hook, supports the work while it's being cut or planed.

The bench hook I favor expands on this basic design. On the right side of the platform I cut a wide rabbet that serves two functions: First, it protects my workbench from being damaged when I use the jig to crosscut material with a backsaw. Second, it guides a handplane when the bench hook is used as a shooting board. I use this feature often to square and true up end grain after crosscutting.

The bench hook is handy for working tenon shoulders and cheeks, but I get further use from it with a thick auxiliary platform, which raises the work surface to about $\frac{1}{8}$ in. below the planing stop. In this configuration I can plane small, thin pieces such as loose tenons or splines.

I also have a second, narrow hook, which I use with the standard bench hook to steady long stock. Both hooks are the same thickness, and the stop on the narrow hook is set the same distance from the leading edge as it is on the standard hook.

Use solid, stable materials

Because I use the bench hook so often in my day-to-day work, I made it from $\frac{7}{8}$-in.-thick hard maple, which is relatively stable. For larger bench hooks you might consider using thicker stock. Quartersawn lumber is ideal, if available, because it's more stable than plainsawn stock.

I also cut dadoes in the platform where the hook and the stop block attach, to ensure that they hold steady and remain perpendicular to the edge of the platform.

Standard bench hook

This bench hook excels at holding stock when crosscutting as well as handplaning. An extension arm adds support for long stock, and an auxiliary deck can be used for planing thin stock.

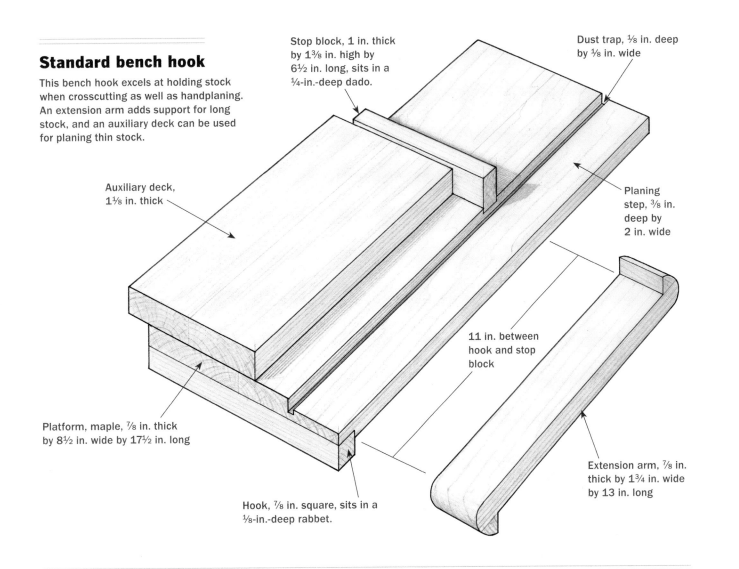

Stop block, 1 in. thick by 1⅜ in. high by 6½ in. long, sits in a ¼-in.-deep dado.

Dust trap, ⅛ in. deep by ⅛ in. wide

Auxiliary deck, 1⅛ in. thick

Planing step, ⅜ in. deep by 2 in. wide

11 in. between hook and stop block

Platform, maple, ⅞ in. thick by 8½ in. wide by 17½ in. long

Hook, ⅞ in. square, sits in a ⅛-in.-deep rabbet.

Extension arm, ⅞ in. thick by 1¾ in. wide by 13 in. long

Hook one end over the workbench. The bench hook makes easy work of cutting the shoulder on a tenon (above). The step on the edge of the bench hook provides a true and square surface to guide a bench plane for trimming the end of a board (right).

An auxiliary deck raises thin stock. A solid-maple shim reduces the relative height of the stop block to accommodate thin stock.

I find one other detail about my bench hook useful. I cut a small groove in the interior corner of the planing step to collect sawdust that accumulates when trimming with a plane. The groove eliminates potential inaccuracies that could be caused by a buildup of sawdust between the jig and the plane.

Two bench hooks for miters

I prefer to cut and fit small bits of molding right at the bench. The precision this method affords is hard to beat: It cuts down on trips across the shop floor to the miter saw or tablesaw, and I've found it to be the safest way to handle small and fragile pieces of molding. To make perfect miters consistently, I use a pair of bench hooks: a miter block for rough-cutting, and a miter shooting board for fine-tuning.

A miter block is a version of the bench hook designed to guide a sawcut at a 45-degree angle in two directions. It serves as a simple version of a miter box. I made mine of solid alder. On the miter block, the hook and stop block are attached to the platform with a dado, similar to the standard bench hook.

There's only one secret to the miter block, and that's setting the 45-degree kerfs in the fence to guide a backsaw. Lay out the kerfs with pencil lines and cut them by hand with a backsaw. Just make sure that the kerfs aren't any wider than the blade on the handsaw you plan to use with the jig, or sloppy miters will result.

Miter shooting board finishes the job

Cuts made at the miter block generally are rough. So I use a second bench hook—a miter shooting board—to tune miters to a perfect 45 degrees. I made mine from two stacked pieces of ⅝-in.-thick Baltic-birch plywood, which is relatively stable. I glued a strip of hardwood in the location of the planing step, which allows me to true up the jig after construction without having to use a handplane on plywood.

Like my other workbench accessories, the shooting board is designed to hook the edge of the bench during use. However, it requires

Miter block

Designed for rough-cutting miters, the miter block is a combination of a bench hook and a miter box. Forward pressure keeps it steady on the bench while the workpiece is held tight against the stop block, and the sawkerfs guide the sawblade.

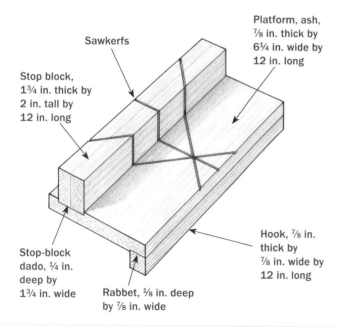

Sawkerfs

Platform, ash, ⅞ in. thick by 6¼ in. wide by 12 in. long

Stop block, 1¾ in. thick by 2 in. tall by 12 in. long

Hook, ⅞ in. thick by ⅞ in. wide by 12 in. long

Stop-block dado, ¼ in. deep by 1¾ in. wide

Rabbet, ⅛ in. deep by ⅞ in. wide

Rough-cut miters. The miter-block bench hook is convenient for cutting small pieces of trim or molding.

a hook on both ends because the jig is designed to be reversed for trimming miters in opposite directions. My shooting board sits on the bench at a tilt, which isn't a problem; however, you can make it long enough to straddle the bench.

Two fences set at 45 degrees (together forming a 90-degree angle) are secured to the platform with glue and screws. Care should be taken to ensure that the fences are accurate, because they serve as a reference for all subsequent cuts made at the shooting board.

A step rabbeted into the edge of the shooting board, as on my standard bench hook, is used to guide a handplane. It also has a small groove for dust accumulation.

When using the miter shooting board, I generally align the layout line of the miter with the end of the fence on the shooting board. Any material that extends into the path of the plane will be trimmed off. Hold the stock snug against the fence, and pass the plane over the stock with repeated strokes until it stops cutting.

Other tips for using a shooting board

To keep a plane cutting smoothly on a shooting board, apply wax to all of the working surfaces of the plane and bench hook. It also is important that the plane's side be perpendicular to the sole and that you tune up the plane correctly for the task. Align the plane blade parallel with its sole, and adjust it for a light cut. Always make sure the side of the plane is firmly registered on the planing step.

When trimming harsh end grain, which tends to dull the blade rapidly, dampen the end grain with water prior to planing.

How much should you cut? Any material that extends beyond the stop block will be trimmed away. Use your layout lines as a guide.

A second bench hook. A miter shooting board tunes miters to a perfect 45 degrees.

Miter shooting board

Sawn miters often require fine-tuning. That's where the miter shooting board comes in handy. Two 45-degree fences made of hardwood support the workpiece as it is trimmed with a jack plane.

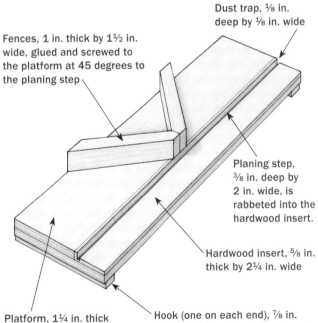

Dust trap, ⅛ in. deep by ⅛ in. wide

Fences, 1 in. thick by 1½ in. wide, glued and screwed to the platform at 45 degrees to the planing step

Planing step, ⅜ in. deep by 2 in. wide, is rabbeted into the hardwood insert.

Hardwood insert, ⅝ in. thick by 2¼ in. wide

Platform, 1¼ in. thick (two pieces of ⅝-in.-thick Baltic-birch plywood) by 7 in. wide by 24 in. long

Hook (one on each end), ⅞ in. thick by ½ in. wide, is glued and screwed to the underside of the platform.

Installing a Cast-Iron Vise

TOM BEGNAL

It's hard to imagine working in a shop that lacks a good bench-mounted vise. After all, woodworkers come from the factory with just two hands, and we need both of them to use most tools. So it usually takes some help to keep a workpiece fixed firmly in place.

The cast-iron style of vise has long been a staple in woodworkers' shops, and for good reason. A cast-iron vise that's well maintained can last several generations, and a workpiece locked in its grip won't easily budge. A cast-iron vise has another plus: It generally installs without much fuss. But that doesn't mean the procedure is foolproof. To minimize the fussiness factor, there are a few worthwhile points to keep in mind—including a little pre-installation planning.

Where to put it

At first glance, a workbench seems to offer a number of places to locate a vise. But a few spots can be eliminated quickly. Any vise centered on the front, back, or end of a bench is sure to be in your way, so the vise almost always ends up installed near a corner to make it as unobtrusive as possible. Your options narrow even further when you consider the bench location, its design, and you—or more specifically, your handedness.

Bench location and design

When a bench is positioned well away from the walls, allowing all-around access, the vise can be installed adjacent to any of the corners. But if the bench butts against a wall, both corners of that side of the bench are eliminated as options. If the bench has to go in a corner, the options become fewer. So it's best not to finalize the vise location until you've considered where the bench is going to go.

Most cast-iron vises have a metal dog built into the front jaw. When the vise dog is used with a benchdog, the vise offers additional clamping advantages. Keep in mind, though, that the holes for the bench-dog must be in line with the vise dog. So before you settle on a vise location, make sure the benchdog you use can be placed into all of the holes without interfering with the vise, the bench legs, or anything else under the top.

Front or end vise?

A vise can be mounted to the front or end of a bench. Because each location has its advantages, many benches include both front and end vises. If a bench is limited to having just one vise, it's best to install it as a front vise, because most of us naturally gravitate toward the front of the bench.

Think right or left

More than anything else, your handedness determines the best vise location. Right-handers usually like a front vise on the left of the bench. That way, when crosscutting

End vise. Used with a benchdog, an end vise allows a longer board to be clamped quickly face-down on the bench for planing, scraping, or sanding.

Front vise. If you're going to mount only one vise, a front vise offers the most useful clamping options. A board clamped horizontally in a front vise is perfectly positioned for edge-planing. Clamp it vertically, and the end of the board can be planed or sawed easily.

Determine the best location

Before installing a vise, consider where on the benchtop it's going to work best for you. Right-handers generally prefer the front vise on the left end of the benchtop, with the end vise on the right, near the front corner. Reverse the locations if you're a southpaw.

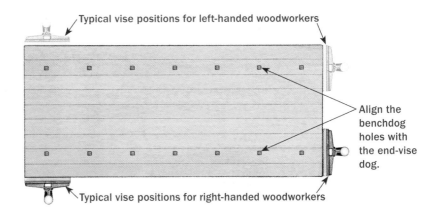

Typical vise positions for left-handed woodworkers

Align the benchdog holes with the end-vise dog.

Typical vise positions for right-handed woodworkers

Figure out the filler-block thickness. With both the vise and benchtop upside down to make the job easier, measure the distance from the benchtop to the top edge of the vise jaws and then add ½ in. to ¾ in.

Attach the filler block, then the vise, using lag screws. You might think that about does it, but to get the most out of the vise, you should cover the metal jaws and edge of the bench next.

Mounting the vise

Jaws should be ½ in. to ¾ in. below the work surface.

Benchtop

Filler block

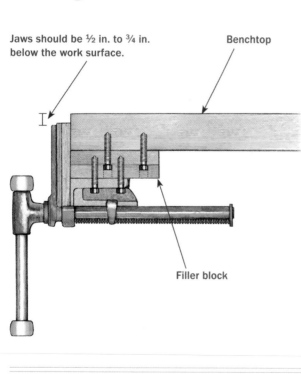

a board with a handsaw, the cutoff end can be held by the left hand.

When the front vise is installed on the left, you'll want the end vise added to the right, near the front corner. Reverse the locations if you're a lefty.

How to mount it

There are several ways to install a cast-iron vise; your best option depends on the benchtop's design. The procedure outlined here covers the most common installation, one where the back jaw of the vise simply butts against the edge of a top that's about 1½ in. thick. Cast-iron vises, especially large ones, are heavy and awkward to hold, so try to work with the benchtop turned upside down, as shown in the top right photo. If flipping the top isn't an option, you can make the vise easier to handle by removing the front jaw along with the screw and guide bars.

A long face. A mortise in the back face accepts the back jaw. The face extends the full length of the benchtop, which will make it easier to clamp long boards.

Include a filler block

Ideally, when the vise is installed, the top edge of the jaws should be ½ in. to ¾ in. below the top of the bench. The extra space allows room for the wood face, added later, to cover the top of the jaw. Also, on some vises, the dog extends almost ½ in. above the jaws, even when the dog is fully lowered. Unless the jaws are well below the benchtop, the dog will always stick above the work surface.

To get that extra space, you're likely to need a wood filler block between the underside of the benchtop and the mounting bracket portion of the vise. The block should be wide and long enough to cover the bracket and thick enough to produce the intended spacing.

Install the filler block and vise

Before securing the block to the underside of the top, drill and counterbore it for four lag screws. Position the block on the benchtop and

Measure, mark, and cut out the mortise. On many vises, the face of the back jaw isn't square to the benchtop. To make sure the mortise ends up deep enough, measure the depth from the thickest part of the jaw (top). Use a drill bit to remove most of the waste stock before using a router to clean out the waste that remains (above).

Plane the top edge of the face. A sharp handplane is all it takes to get the face flush with the top of the bench.

Attach the back face to the edge of the benchtop. To fill in the gap between the back face and the back jaw of the vise, add a couple of strips of epoxy putty to the mortise just before applying the face to the bench (top). After coating the jaw with paste wax, attach the face with a few wood screws driven into counterbored holes (above).

drill the pilot holes. Add glue, then slip the lag screws into the holes and thread them home.

Now position the vise on the block, with the back jaw firmly against the edge of the bench. Then drill the pilot holes and add the lag screws. If you've been working with the benchtop upside down, now's the time to flip it right-side up.

Make wooden faces

A workpiece secured in the vise is less likely to dent if the cast-iron jaws have wood faces. The faces can be installed several ways. A quick method is simply to screw a rectangular piece of hardwood stock to the jaws of the vise. Most jaws have predrilled holes, making the job an easy one. I prefer to mortise the back face to accept the back jaw. Also, I like to extend the back face the full length of the bench. Effectively then, the back face becomes part of the edge of the benchtop. So when a long board is clamped on edge in the vise, the board remains in contact with the back face the full length of the bench. That makes it easier to clamp the end of the board to the benchtop.

To create the mortise, first mark its length, width, and depth on the back of the back face. When measuring the depth, keep in mind that most jaws taper in thickness, meaning the back jaw usually isn't square to the benchtop. So to make sure the jaw can fit fully into the mortise, measure the depth dimension at the bottom of the jaw at its thickest point.

Once the mortise has been marked, use a drill press and a Forstner bit to remove most of the waste. Clean up the rest with a router.

Mount the faces

At this point, there's just one more detail to attend to before the back face can be attached. Because the back jaw is tapered, it doesn't fit fully against the mortise. As a result, there's a gap that widens as it nears the top of the jaw. Thus, the jaw loses some support provided by the back face.

To fill in the gap, use a bit of epoxy in putty form (see the top left photo on the facing page). You can find this stuff at most hardware or home-improvement stores. To prevent the epoxy from sticking to the jaw, add a heavy coat of paste wax to the area of the jaw that meets the epoxy. Next, attach the back face, using the vise to clamp one end. The top edge of the face should stand proud of the benchtop by 1/16 in. Now add a bar clamp to the other end of the face. Secure the face with screws driven into counterbored holes (see the bottom photo on the facing page), and add wood plugs to the holes.

The front face is just rectangular stock that's attached by driving screws through holes in the front jaw. Because the front jaw has a taper, like the back jaw, the front face cants toward the back face. That's actually a plus because it helps the vise grip more tightly along the full width of the jaws. But if there's too much cant, it can be reduced quickly by handplaning a bevel on the entire inside surface of the front face (see the top photo).

For the final step, add a finish to the two faces, preferably one that matches the finish on the original benchtop.

Add the front face. Like the back jaw of the vise, the front jaw is tapered. To minimize the effect of the taper, you can bevel the outside surface of the front face slightly (top). Then attach the face by driving two screws through predrilled holes in the jaw (above).

Bar-Clamp End Vise

MIKE BILLICK

Here's how to add an inexpensive and versatile tail vise to your workbench that can be easily removed when you need to save space. Mount two ¾-in.-dia. pipe flanges solidly to the undercarriage of the bench. Make two pipe-clamp heads (I used Jorgensen style No. 50) on short sections of pipe and screw the pipes into the flanges to make the vise. On my bench I added some thickness to the top to create a deeper clamping jaw. I also screwed hardwood clamping pads to each clamp head. The clamping pads are sized so that they are normally flush with the top of the bench; but when rotated 90 degrees, the pads extend ⅝ in. above the top of the bench. This allows the vise to hold, in conjunction with benchdogs, large panels flat on the benchtop for routing.

I also purchased two additional clamp heads (Jorgensen style No. 56). These sliding heads, when combined with various lengths of pipe, make the vise more versatile by increasing the size range of workpieces it can hold.

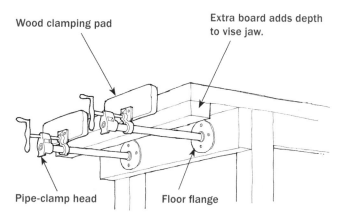

Wood clamping pad

Extra board adds depth to vise jaw.

Pipe-clamp head

Floor flange

In normal position the vise clamping pad is flush with the benchtop.

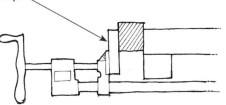

When rotated 90 degrees the vise clamping pad stands above the benchtop.

Benchdog

Holding Carvings Securely

FREDERICK WILBUR

For the aspiring wood-carver and professional alike, a carving station is an uncomplicated way to hold a workpiece steady as you carve. The use of a large board with various ways to grip the work is nothing new, but this smaller version is easy to make and extremely versatile. You need only a piece of smooth and dense plywood, 14 in. by 28 in., and scraps of plywood and hardwood.

Different sides of the board adapt to different tasks

One side of the board has fences and various filler strips that hold irregularly shaped workpieces in place with the help of a pair of wedges or cams. The flat side can hold a flat-backed blank screwed in place through the plywood. Mark the length and width centerlines in pencil on the flat side because they will come in handy for locating screws

A portable carving station

The simplicity of this carving station, made from scraps of plywood and lumber, belies its versatility. With a variety of wedges, cam clamps, and standard shop clamps, you can use the carving station to secure a workpiece of any shape to a bench or table.

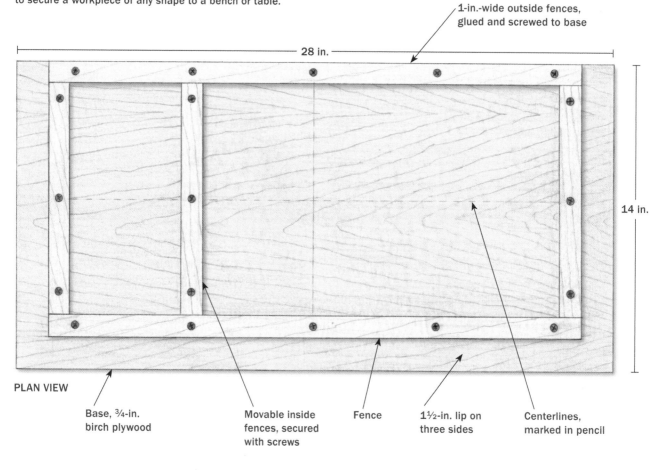

1-in.-wide outside fences, glued and screwed to base

28 in.

14 in.

PLAN VIEW

Base, ¾-in. birch plywood

Movable inside fences, secured with screws

Fence

1½-in. lip on three sides

Centerlines, marked in pencil

Wedges work wonders. Using opposing wedges as clamps is a technique familiar to many woodworkers. In an application such as the one shown here, cut the wedges from stock thicker than the ¾-in. fence material to facilitate removal.

Eccentric cam clamps are quick and sturdy. Secure an irregularly shaped corbel by screwing a movable fence to the base. Against that fence two cam clamps rotate, pushing against another, loose fence that presses against a scrap from the bandsawn corbel. Add a cushion of foam rubber to prevent marring the workpiece.

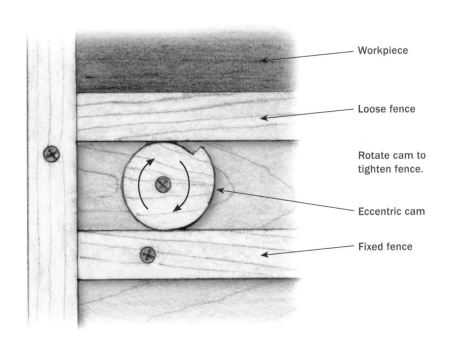

Workpiece

Loose fence

Rotate cam to tighten fence.

Eccentric cam

Fixed fence

Use both sides of the base. When carving blanks with flat backs, screw the blank to the base of the carving station (left) to hold it in place. Take care to locate screws where they will not damage carving tools (above).

Small rosettes need some extra care. To hold really small workpieces such as these rosettes firmly in place as he carves them, the author drills shallow holes in a scrap of plywood. A piece of double-faced tape on the back of each rosette keeps it from slipping around in its hole.

and aligning blanks. Also, for work that has symmetrically curved silhouettes, you can draw a system of grid lines on the plywood.

On the side that has four fences screwed and glued to it, place three of the fences set in from the edges by 1½ in. or so. Set the fourth fence flush with the edge of the plywood base. The longer inset fence provides a long edge that is perfect for holding pieces of molding in place, and the flanges created on the shorter sides allow you to secure the carving station to a bench or table.

Many wood-carvers who do detailed work prefer to carve on a slanted surface so that they can see the workpiece clearly without having to lean over. I made an angled easel that fits snugly into the fence side of the carving station. The ends are two 30-degree/60-degree right triangles made of ¾-in. plywood, connected by two rectangular pieces that overlap the triangles. The triangles are located to fit between the short fences on the base. I also notched out the ends to fit over the two long fences.

Two ways to hold moldings. A fence set back from the edge of the base leaves a perfect space to support long pieces of molding, which the author clamps in place using scraps of wood cut to the shape of the molding and cushioned with foam rubber padding (right). Shorter, mitered pieces can be locked in place with mitered cleats that are screwed or clamped to the base (left).

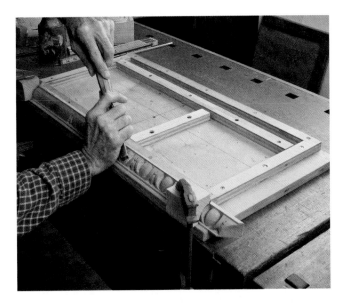

A drop-in easel for more comfort. An angled easel places workpieces at a more comfortable height and angle. The four bottom corners are notched to fit within the fences on the base (above), and the easel is held in place by its own weight. Lips on the top outside edges allow for clamps to hold some workpieces in place (left); others can be secured with screws from behind.

Tune Up Your Workbench

RICHARD L. HUMPHREVILLE

Even after 30 years as a cabinet-maker, I still vividly remember the painstaking effort it took to build my first professional workbench. The finished bench was a thing of beauty, and at first I was reluctant to use it, showing it off to anyone who walked into my shop. When I did start using it, the inevitable first ding made me cringe.

But damage to a workbench is impossible to avoid. After years of hard use as a platform for sawing, planing, chiseling, hammering, pounding, gluing, and finishing, any bench, no matter how elegant, will need some careful restoration.

I've revived a number of war-scarred and battle-weary benches over the years. Bench designs differ, but all benefit from a flat top, rigid base, and well-tuned vises. I'll show you how to bring back any kind of bench to the perfect working condition that befits the most important tool in your shop.

TLC for your workbench

You can't do good work on a worn-out bench, so flatten the top, tighten the base, and adjust the vises.

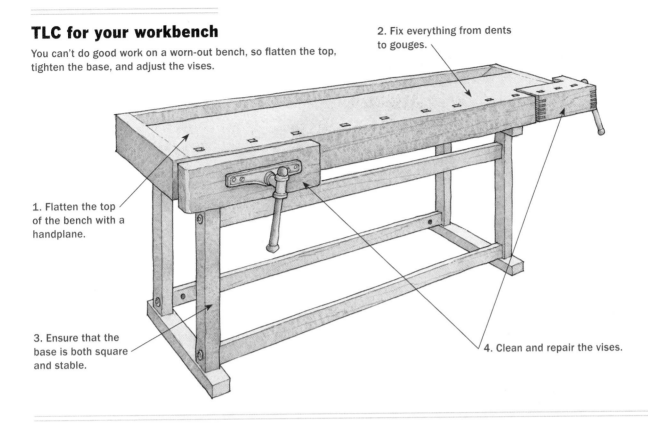

2. Fix everything from dents to gouges.

1. Flatten the top of the bench with a handplane.

3. Ensure that the base is both square and stable.

4. Clean and repair the vises.

Prepare your benchtop for flattening

Use a card scraper or cabinet scraper to remove any glue, paint, or other gunk that's built up on the top surface and edges. After the top is clean, use a pair of winding sticks to check for twist in the benchtop, marking any high spots that will need to be removed. Then use a 4-ft. ruler or straightedge to see where the top has lost its flatness. Drag the ruler's edge lengthwise across the width and diagonally over the entire top, highlighting all the high spots with a pencil.

Next, take off the vises and put them aside to be tuned up later. If your bench has stabilizing battens at each end, unbolt them and clean out any sawdust buildup on both halves of the joint. Put the battens aside, too.

Smooth the bumps. Use a scraper to remove any dried glue or finish from the benchtop.

Twist detective. A pair of winding sticks allows you to see if the benchtop is twisted.

Flag the high spots. Move the edge of a 4-ft. ruler across the benchtop and use a pencil to mark the high areas.

Remove the vises. You'll tune up the vises after the top has been flattened. If your bench has them, unbolt the stabilizing battens (right) and clean out any sawdust that has worked its way down between them and the benchtop.

Pick a number. To flatten the benchtop, you can use (from left) a No. 5 plane (bevel up or bevel down), a No. 6, or a No. 7. The plane's length should nearly equal the width of the benchtop (excluding any tool tray).

Bevel the edge. To prevent tearout when handplaning across the benchtop, use a block plane to create a small chamfer along the back edge.

Handplane your benchtop

Early in my career, I used a belt sander to flatten my bench, but it only made matters worse. Handplaning is the way to go. You'll need a well-tuned No. 5, No. 6, or No. 7 plane, depending on the size of the workbench (see photo at left). A high-quality plane from Lie-Nielsen or Veritas is a major investment, but you can buy less expensive planes from Stanley® or Anant. It is also possible to find used planes on eBay® or at flea markets, or you can borrow one from a fellow woodworker. Planing the benchtop will be physically demanding and is not a task for those in poor shape. Traditionally, teenage apprentices were given the job on a cool day.

Adjust the plane to take thin shavings, which will minimize tearout and keep you from overexerting yourself. With the plane at a slight skew to the direction of travel, begin the planing sequence (see "Flatten your benchtop in three steps" on the facing page) with passes across the width of the benchtop. Overlap the previous pass just enough to avoid leaving unplaned strips. Work the plane across the entire surface in one direction and then the other, being careful to avoid rounding over the front and rear edges of the bench surface. Making this mistake prolongs the flattening process.

Flatten your benchtop in three steps

Begin by planing perpendicular to the benchtop, overlapping each stroke and slightly skewing the plane (1). Then work your way up and down the top, planing in a diagonal direction (2). Finally, plane along the length of the benchtop, altering direction to match the grain of individual boards (3).

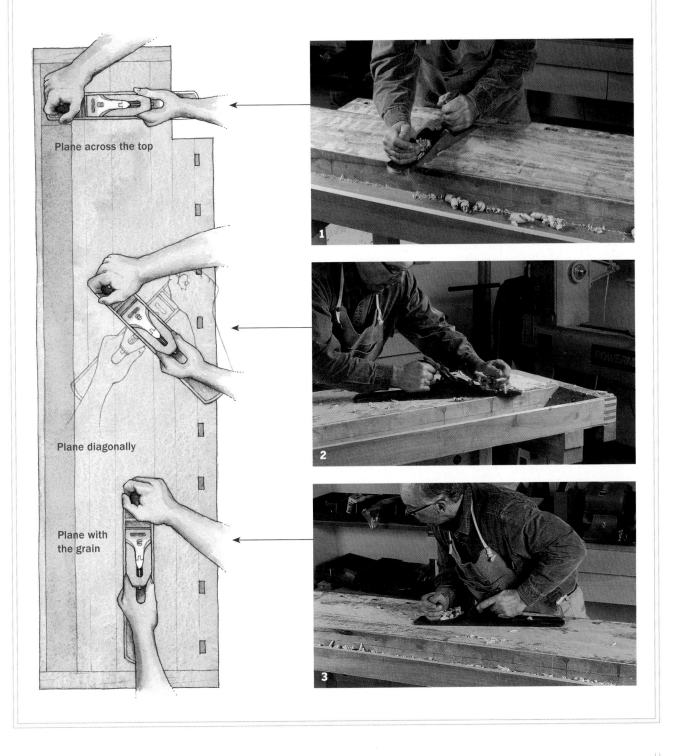

Plane across the top

Plane diagonally

Plane with the grain

A Dutchman to the rescue.
Lay a piece of wood (known as a "Dutchman") over a damaged section of the top and mark around it. Chisel out this section (left). Apply glue to two sides of the patch and insert it into the benchtop (below). The dovetail shape gives mechanical strength when patching an edge.

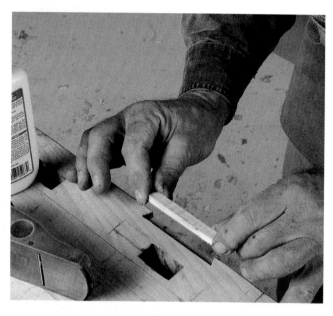

Square pegs in round holes.
After cleaning up small holes with a Forstner bit, cut a peg slightly larger than the hole. Taper two opposite sides of the peg, round its corners (above left), and tap it into the hole (above right). When the glue has dried, trim the plug flush (right).

The next sequence is to plane the surface diagonally from left to right and then right to left. Again, this process is very deliberate and must be done with care to flatten the bench surface thoroughly. Last, plane the length of the bench, switching directions if necessary to go with the grain of individual boards.

Once this sequence of planing passes is complete, check your progress with the straightedge. This time, mark the low spots with a pencil. Usually, you'll need to plane the surface several times using this sequence before it is flat, so keep the plane blade razor-sharp and pace yourself.

Repair any holes or dents in the top

After verifying that the benchtop is flat by sweeping the straightedge over the surface in all directions, use a cabinet scraper to remove any ridges, or tracks, left by the handplane.

Even with a flat surface, there will be gouges and holes too deep to be removed by planing. To patch deep gouges, I use a "Dutchman," which is a piece of wood slightly deeper, wider, and longer than the gouge and of the same species and appearance as the benchtop. Lay the Dutchman over the gouge with the grain aligned, then use a marking knife to scribe a line around it. Next use a router, laminate trimmer, or chisel to remove the wood from the benchtop within the scribe lines. A pressure fit with no gaps around the edges is your goal. To make it easier to fit the Dutchman, it helps to chamfer its leading edges lightly. After gluing the Dutchman in place, use a plane to bring it flush with the benchtop.

Smaller holes require a simpler approach. First, clean up the hole using a Forstner bit. Then cut a square peg slightly larger than the hole, taper two opposite sides at the tip, and round over the corners using a block plane. Put some glue in the hole, align the untapered edges of the peg parallel to the direction of the bench grain to prevent the bench surface from splitting, and tap in the peg. When dry, saw off the protruding part of the peg and chisel the surface flat.

To fill shallow chipouts, mix epoxy with very fine sawdust. A loose mix with a minimum amount of sawdust is best to enable the epoxy to sink thoroughly into the affected areas. You also can add a little dye powder to help match the color of the filler to the bench.

Any small, shallow dents can be steamed out with the tip of an iron. Put some water in the dent, let it stand for a few minutes, and then place a wet cotton rag over the area. Apply the leading inch or two of a hot steam iron over the rag. Keep adding water to the rag as you go. Be persistent; hardwoods like maple and beech are slow to swell when steamed.

If you removed the stabilizing battens, now is the time to reattach them tight against the end grain of the benchtop and flush with the surface, scraping or planing them if needed.

Check for a sturdy and stable base

My experience has shown that a well-constructed bench retains its structural integrity. Nevertheless, a thorough check should be made, so remove the benchtop and see if the base has any joints that need regluing or bolts that need tightening.

If the stretchers are bolted to the legs, tighten them. As you work, use a large T-square and take diagonal measurements to check for square.

On my bench, the legs must have been made while the lumber had a higher moisture level than the upper rails and the feet. As a result, the tenons shrank away from the mortises. In a situation like this, scrape away

Epoxy does it. Medium-size holes can be filled with a mixture of very fine sawdust and epoxy. Frame each hole with masking tape.

A swell repair. Minor dents can be repaired by applying a hot iron to the damp wood, causing the wood to swell.

Reglue loose joints. Epoxy mixed with fine sawdust makes a good gap-filling glue if joints on the base have become loose.

Check for square. When regluing and tightening the base, make sure the structure remains square.

as much dry glue as possible, then carve some grooves on the tenons with a chisel, which gives the epoxy a better mechanical bond with the wood. Because the epoxy will need to fill the gaps, mix in some sawdust (the same mixture used to fill dents in the benchtop). Apply the epoxy and clamp the joints, checking for square as you go.

If your bench has wooden feet that rest on the shop floor, check them to see if they are split or worn down. If so, replace them. After removing any nails or screws, remove the old feet with a handsaw or chisel and mallet. Before attaching new ones, remove the old glue and flatten the surface where they will be attached. Hot vinegar is excellent at loosening most glues, but use a heat gun very carefully to loosen epoxy.

With the new feet glued and screwed (counterbore and bung the holes), I glue on 1/16-in.- to 1/8-in.-thick rubber pads from underlay material available at carpet stores. These help balance the bench, reduce future wear, and keep the bench from sliding around the floor.

To level the benchtop, shim up the low spots where the base is attached.

Nonskid pads. Thin pieces of rubber carpet underlay glued to the bottom of the feet prevent the bench from sliding around in use.

A clean and fresh metal vise. To prevent sticking, clean and lubricate the guide bars and the threaded rod (left). Attach fresh hardwood cheeks to the jaws (below).

Clean and repair the vises

With the rest of the bench finished, the next step is to clean and repair the vises. As the bench ages, the wood shrinks and expands, loosening both bolts and joints and shifting vises out of alignment.

Lubricate the guide bars and threaded rods with a spray lubricant. When you reattach a vise, alignment is critical, so use a straightedge to check that the vise is level with the benchtop and a ruler to verify that the open jaw is parallel to the bench. Keep the attachment bolts snugged up but still loose enough to tap the vise into perfect alignment before the final tightening. Replace worn-out hardwood cheeks on the inner jaws of a metal vise. Be

sure the upper edges of the cheeks touch first, by a fraction of an inch, when closing the jaws.

If your tail vise has adjustment screws on the guide bar, use them to align the vise flush with the benchtop. You may also need to plane joints that have become exposed due to wood shrinkage and now prevent the vise from closing completely.

Sand and seal the benchtop

With the bench reassembled, very lightly sand the top smooth using P220-grit paper. To seal the benchtop, I use two coats of Zinsser's® Bull's Eye amber shellac, thinned with three parts alcohol to one part shellac. I prefer shellac to a coat of oil because it seals the wood more thoroughly and reduces seasonal movement. Gently sand between each coat with P320-grit paper, apply some paste wax using 0000 steel wool, and buff the surface with a cotton cloth.

When the bench is back in use, frequent light cleanups will keep any long-term wear in check. At the end of each day, when putting away tools and straightening up the shop, look over the bench for any glue or stain and clean it off. This step goes hand in hand with sharpening and maintaining all your other tools.

Level a wood vise. If joints have become proud (left), plane them smooth so that the two faces of the vise can meet seamlessly. Plane the top of the vise flush with that of the benchtop (below).

Seal with shellac. A couple of coats of thinned shellac seal the benchtop better than oil.

A Sliding Bench Jack Holds Boards on Edge at Any Height

ABRAHAM TESSER

To plane a long board on edge, woodworkers often clamp one end in a front vise and support the other end on a device known as a bench jack.

A traditional bench jack is clamped into the tail vise (either L-shaped or full width) and uses a dowel to support the workpiece. The jack often has holes from top to bottom that allow the dowel to be adjusted for different board widths and working heights. This adjustment method is relatively crude and doesn't restrict the board from wobbling from side to side as you plane it. So I came up with this design, which features a sliding shuttle equipped with a toggle clamp (DeStaCo® No. 225-U; www.grainger.com) to hold the board against the bench.

In use, the bench jack rests on the floor and is clamped into the tail vise (for a bench without a tail vise, you might attach the jack permanently). I adjust the shuttle by loosening the knobs and simply sliding it up or down its T-track. Once the height is locked in and the material is resting on the shuttle, I flip the toggle clamp. The toggle clamp can be adjusted to accept materials as thin as the shuttle (¾ in. in this case) or up to almost an inch thicker. If the workpiece is thinner than the shuttle, I add a spacer between the clamp head and the workpiece.

With the workpiece supported and clamped into the jack, it is ready for planing, shaping, or sanding. The material will be held firmly at the desired height with much less side-to-side movement.

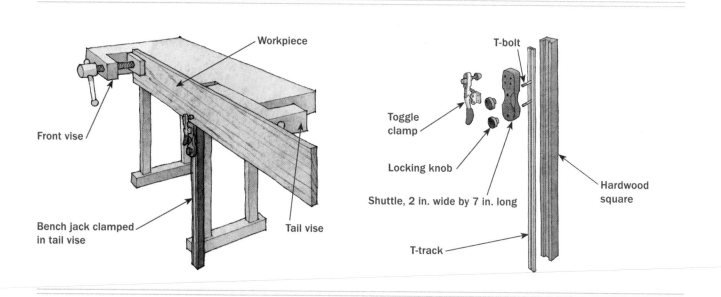

Workpiece

Front vise

Bench jack clamped in tail vise

Tail vise

T-bolt

Toggle clamp

Locking knob

Shuttle, 2 in. wide by 7 in. long

Hardwood square

T-track

Pipe-Clamp Parts Make a Workbench More Versatile

DANIEL THOMAS

While drilling dog holes in my new maple benchtop, I realized that ¾ in. is the tap drill size for a ½-in. pipe thread. After drilling the dog holes to size, I tapped them with a ½-in. pipe tap, going deeper than the normal thread depth for a pipe to give the threads more holding strength in wood. This allowed me to screw a threaded section of ½-in.-dia. pipe into the tapped dog hole and, in turn, screw a pipe-clamp head to the pipe's other end. I've been using this setup for two years now, and the tapped wooden threads in the hard maple have held up just fine in their double duty as dog hole and threaded insert.

I use the threaded dog holes in three ways: First, I can install a clamp perpendicular to the benchtop in any dog hole to use as a hold-down. Second, after drilling and tapping holes in the apron of the bench, I can use a clamp as a side vise against a dog. Finally, utilizing drilled and tapped holes on the opposite side of the apron, I can attach the quick-release end of the pipe clamp. This lets me hold items that are wider than the benchtop.

The tapped holes on the side of my bench are really neat—it is like having an extra vise. You can screw a short or long pipe into the hole. The arrangement gives a lot of latitude for clamping. When locating the side holes, it is important to put them at the correct height below the top of the bench—too low and the clamp head will not be above the top of the bench.

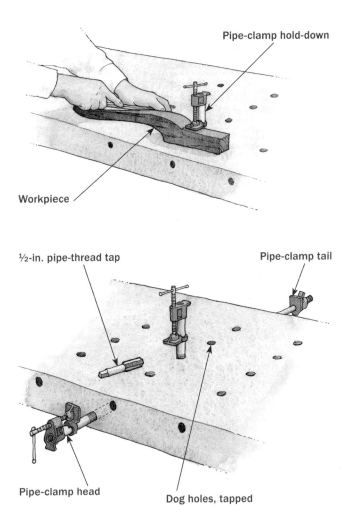

Pipe-clamp hold-down

Workpiece

½-in. pipe-thread tap

Pipe-clamp tail

Pipe-clamp head

Dog holes, tapped

A Rolling Lift for Your Workbench

TIM JANSSEN

When I built my workbench, I didn't skimp on materials. As a result, the bench weighs around 300 lb. Because my shop is small, I occasionally need to move the beast—not an easy task for one person.

To make life easier, I came up with this design for a rolling lift, which uses wood scraps, a small car jack (picked up at the scrap yard), four heavy-duty swivel casters, and six butt hinges.

The mechanism consists of two lift plates made from plywood and 2×6s, attached to the bench legs with hinges. Two casters are secured to the base of each lift plate. A 2×4 crossbar, attached to the lift plates with hinges, lifts the bench onto the casters when the car jack is opened. Closing the jack drops the bench onto its own legs. The mechanism is simple but effective.

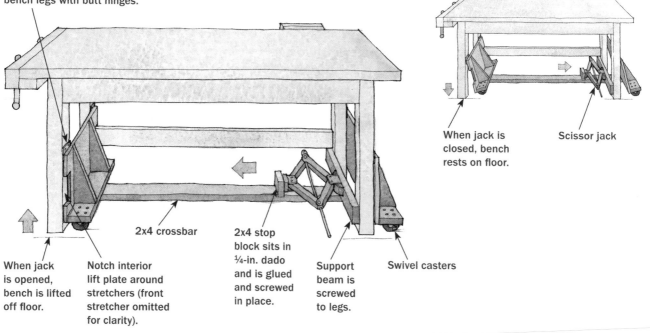

Lift plates attached to crossbar and bench legs with butt hinges.

When jack is opened, bench is lifted off floor.

Notch interior lift plate around stretchers (front stretcher omitted for clarity).

2x4 crossbar

2x4 stop block sits in ¼-in. dado and is glued and screwed in place.

Support beam is screwed to legs.

Swivel casters

When jack is closed, bench rests on floor.

Scissor jack

Workbench Extension Lengthens Clamping Capacity

AURELIO BOLOGNESI

A few years ago, one of my customers wanted a 12-ft.-long tapered flagpole. My plan was to make an octagonal blank and then use a handplane to shape it into a tapered cylinder. But the pole was 5 ft. longer than my bench, and that introduced a clamping problem.

My solution was this workbench extension that effectively lengthened clamping capacity by several feet. Now that I have the extension, I use it whenever I have a workpiece longer than my bench, such as bedposts, tabletops, and countertops.

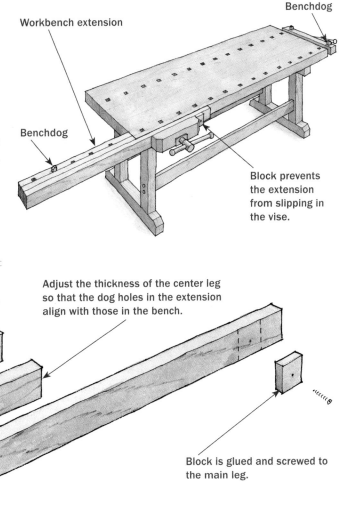

Workbench extension

Benchdog

Benchdog

Block prevents the extension from slipping in the vise.

Dadoes in the outside leg create holes for the benchdog.

Outside 2×6 leg, 5 ft. long

Adjust the thickness of the center leg so that the dog holes in the extension align with those in the bench.

Block is glued and screwed to the main leg.

Main 2×6 leg, 7 ft. long

Adjustable Support for a Workbench

JOS MERTENS

From my own experience I know how important it is to put work at the right height. This goes not only for the workbench itself but also for everything that you do on it. For example, when you want to plane the edge of a shelf, it is important to have it at just the right height—too low will wear out your back, and too high will wear out your arms.

To put work at the right height, we Dutch use an adjustable support called a *knecht,* which translates to "helping boy." To eliminate some inherent problems in the traditional knecht design, which is freestanding, I modified it so that the upright fits into the dog holes in a traditional European-style workbench. The device is so useful that I find myself using it every day for many purposes: gluing, routing, sanding, and planing.

To make the support, first cut the hardwood upright for a loose fit in your benchdog holes. Although the upright looks fragile, it can handle several hundred pounds of weight easily. Next, drill a series of ¼-in.-dia. holes every 1½ in. or so near the back edge of the upright. With a bandsaw, open up each hole at an angle of 45 degrees. Cut the work holder from stock that is the same thickness as the upright, and then make the catch mechanism from aluminum bar stock and a couple of bolts. Finally, glue a piece of carpeting to the top of the holder so that your workpiece won't be damaged.

To use the device, remove the work holder and slip the upright into a dog hole from the top. Slip the work holder back on the upright and, using the catch, set the height of the work holder for the job at hand. If you have a long workpiece to support, you may need two or even three of these fixtures.

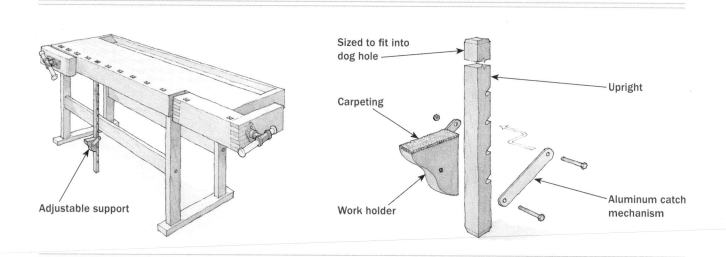

Adjustable support

Sized to fit into dog hole

Carpeting

Work holder

Upright

Aluminum catch mechanism

A Benchtop Bench

JEFF MILLER

Woodworking benches are designed to place a workpiece at a height that's ideal for handplaning. But the perfect height for planing often is too low for other common bench tasks. For example, when routing, carving, cutting dovetails, or doing layout, I frequently have found myself bent over at an uncomfortable angle so that I could see clearly and work effectively. When performing these tasks, I like to have a workpiece positioned 6 in. to 10 in. above my waist level.

To bring a workpiece to my ideal height range, I made a small workbench that mounts quickly to my regular bench. When extra height is needed, the minibench effectively raises the work surface to my comfort zone. The bench is easy to move, stores nicely under my bigger bench, and includes a vise that provides plenty of holding force. I made the bench out of maple, but any hard, dense wood will work.

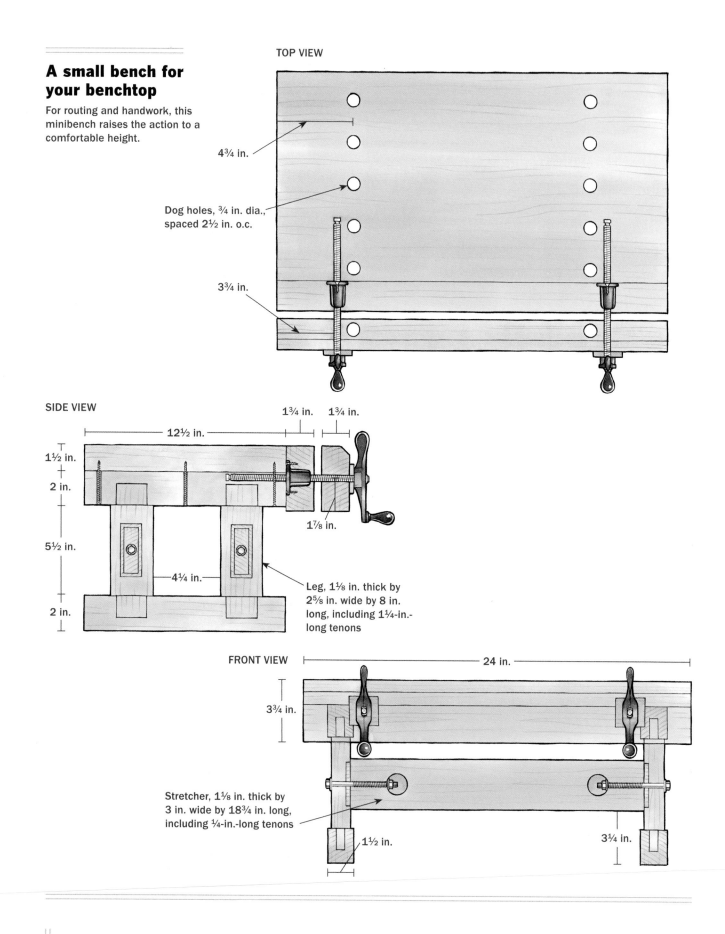

A small bench for your benchtop

For routing and handwork, this minibench raises the action to a comfortable height.

TOP VIEW

4¾ in.

Dog holes, ¾ in. dia., spaced 2½ in. o.c.

3¾ in.

SIDE VIEW

1¾ in.   1¾ in.

12½ in.

1½ in.

2 in.

5½ in.

4¼ in.

1⅞ in.

2 in.

Leg, 1⅛ in. thick by 2⅝ in. wide by 8 in. long, including 1¼-in.-long tenons

FRONT VIEW   24 in.

3¾ in.

Stretcher, 1⅛ in. thick by 3 in. wide by 18¾ in. long, including ¼-in.-long tenons

1½ in.

3¼ in.

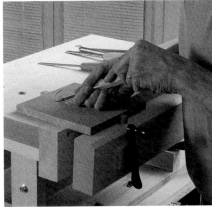

Elevated bench saves your back. This benchtop bench elevates a workpiece several inches above a regular workbench, so it is more comfortable to do such tasks as cutting, carving, and routing.

Trestle design is simple yet strong

I wanted the benchtop bench to be as sturdy as my regular bench. I settled on a trestle-table design, which ensured a solid bench and simplified construction.

Begin by making the top. It can be sized to suit individual needs, but as a general rule, keep the top small enough to be moved without back strain. Joint and edge-glue the stock, then use a handplane and scraper to level and smooth the surfaces. Cut the piece to width and length.

Next, mill the stock for the trestle base. I chose a mortise-and-tenon joint to connect the legs to the aprons and feet, but half-lap joints would work well, too. Cut mortises in the aprons and feet for the legs, then cut shallow mortises centered on the inside faces of the legs to locate and solidify the bolted joints with the stretchers. Cut and fit the tenons on the legs and the stretchers. The stretcher tenons will not be glued, so it's especially important that they fit without any slop. Now

is a good time to drill the ⅜-in.-dia. bolt holes centered on the legs.

The trestle base is screwed to the top through three countersunk holes in the bottom of each apron. Elongate the center and rear holes to allow for the expansion and contraction of the top (see the center drawing on the facing page). To glue up the trestles, spread glue in the mortises and very lightly on the tenons, push the parts together, then clamp up. Check for square and adjust, if necessary.

The stretchers need to be drilled for the bolts that will hold the base together. Use the bolt holes in the trestle legs as drill guides. Dry-assemble the base and clamp it together, but leave access to the bolt holes. Be sure to drill to depth straight; use a self-centering dowel jig, if you need to.

Mark the locations for the hex-nut access holes on the inside faces of the stretchers. Drill with a 1¼-in.-dia. Forstner bit to within 3⁄16 in. of the outside face of each stretcher. The hex nuts and washers go into these holes.

Base assembly

The trestles and stretchers are assembled using mortise-and-tenon construction, giving the benchtop bench solid framing.

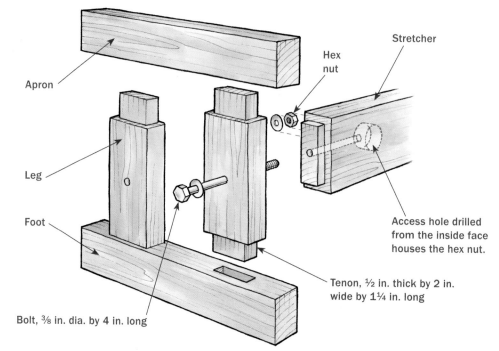

Apron

Leg

Foot

Hex nut

Stretcher

Access hole drilled from the inside face houses the hex nut.

Tenon, ½ in. thick by 2 in. wide by 1¼ in. long

Bolt, ⅜ in. dia. by 4 in. long

Glue up the trestles, then attach the stretchers. A long bolt connects the end of each stretcher to the trestles. Note the access hole in the stretcher.

Vise adds versatility

The front vise makes it easy to clamp a workpiece either to the front of the bench or on top of it. Although I wanted the vise to be simple and easy to make, I also needed it to accept wide boards for dovetailing carcases. As it turned out, a couple of veneer-press screws satisfied both requirements.

Mill the vise jaw and the bench face to their designated thicknesses, then cut them to the same width and length. Mark the locations for the veneer-press-screw holes on the inside of the bench face. Clamp the vise jaw and bench face together and drill through the bench face into the jaw with a ⅛-in.-dia. drill bit. This hole helps align the hole for the veneer-press nut with the one for the screw. Check the dimensions of the veneer-press screws. I used a (roughly) ⅝-in.-dia. screw, with the outside of the veneer-press nut measuring about 1 in. dia., although it tapered slightly. Drill the hole for the screw in the vise jaw and the hole for the nut in the bench face. The end plate that comes with each screw will not be used. You can remove the plate simply by loosening the mounting screw.

Enlarge the hole for the veneer-press nut, concentrating on the end of the hole nearest the benchtop. Tap the nut into place to check your progress. (The paint on the nut will rub off when it is tapped in place, leaving a clear picture of the areas that need relief.) You can remove the nut by threading the veneer-press screw into place and then tapping the end of the screw (not the handle) with a mallet.

Once the nut fits, trace the outline of the flange onto the inside of the bench face. Rout away enough wood to allow the nut, and the screws that will attach it to the face, to sit flush with or slightly below the surface. Screw the nuts into place.

Clamp the bench face into position so that the top edge is flush with the benchtop, and screw the two outermost screws into

Inset the veneer-press nuts into the back of the bench face. Trace the flange profile (top) and rout a recess to set the nut flush with the stock. Secure with screws (above).

Vise assembly

Before attaching the bench face to the benchtop, drill the holes for the veneer-press screws and install the hardware. The screws will close the vise jaw, but you'll have to pull it open manually.

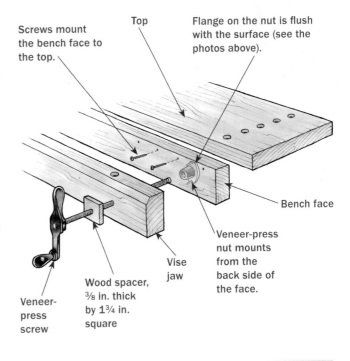

Screws mount the bench face to the top.

Top

Flange on the nut is flush with the surface (see the photos above).

Bench face

Veneer-press nut mounts from the back side of the face.

Vise jaw

Wood spacer, ⅜ in. thick by 1¾ in. square

Veneer-press screw

Attach the base. Mount the top to the base by driving three screws through holes (two slotted, one round) in each apron.

place (drill and countersink pilot holes first). Turn over the benchtop and check where the veneer-press screw will come through the face. Depending on the size of your bench, you may have to rout a channel on the underside of the benchtop for the veneer-press screw. Mark exactly where the channel will be, then remove the bench face to rout the channel. Reattach the face, and try to thread the vise screw into place. Remove more wood as necessary.

The veneer-press-screw handles will need more clearance to operate easily. Glue wooden spacers, roughly ⅜ in. thick by 1¾ in. square, over the veneer-press-screw holes. Run the bit you used to drill these holes through the spacers from inside the jaw. The vise jaw will not open automatically when you loosen the veneer-press screws. You can pull it open manually, or refine the vise with two modified ⅝-in. drill-bit stop collars or

shaft collars. The bore of the collars might have to be enlarged to fit on the veneer-press screw. A machine shop can do this for you, or you can file it by hand.

Benchdogs boost performance

The addition of Veritas Bench Pups® allows me to hold a workpiece on top of the bench. Lay out the positions for holes in the benchtop and the vise jaw, being careful to avoid the area over the veneer-press screws and the apron of the base. Bore ¾-in.-dia. holes and insert the Bench Pups. The benchtop holes are best drilled on the drill press, with the bench face removed.

Reattach the face when everything is positioned properly and works smoothly. Apply glue to the mating surfaces, then add the screws. Finally, mount the base to the top by driving screws through the holes in the aprons.

An Adjustable-Height Worktable on Wheels

BOB BELLEVILLE

After several years and many projects, I'm still finding new uses for this rolling, adjustable-height worktable. The latticework top, made from 2×4s and assembled with biscuits, is a versatile aid for glue-ups and assembly work, and it can be raised or lowered as needed. I typically lower it for assembling cabinets and raise it to save my back for detail work, like cleaning up dovetails.

The top can be adjusted from 24 in. to 38 in. tall via four risers that fit through openings in the top of the base cabinet. Over-size knobs and plywood blocks lock and unlock the risers. Each knob has a captive ⅜-in. nut that connects to a ⅜-in. bolt threaded through the block and riser slot. A glued-in dowel prevents the block from pivoting in the slot. Each riser is marked in 1-in. increments to make it easy to level the top.

Clamps can be placed anywhere on the top, both vertically and horizontally, to glue up small and medium pieces or secure work for power sanding. I also clamp scrap lumber to the top to create impromptu stops and holders for speeding up repetitive work such as routing, pocket-screw joinery, or biscuit-slot cutting.

The top of the base cabinet helps prevent the cart from racking and provides a temporary resting place for tools and hardware. A pair of hardware-store wheels on a simple ½-in. axle makes it easy to move the table wheelbarrow style.

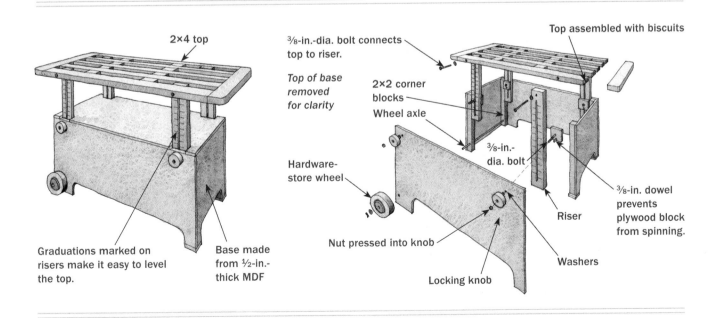

2×4 top

Graduations marked on risers make it easy to level the top.

Base made from ½-in.-thick MDF

⅜-in.-dia. bolt connects top to riser.

Top of base removed for clarity

Hardware-store wheel

Nut pressed into knob

Locking knob

Top assembled with biscuits

2×2 corner blocks

Wheel axle

⅜-in.-dia. bolt

Riser

Washers

⅜-in. dowel prevents plywood block from spinning.

A Commercially Available Adjustable Bench

JEFF MILLER

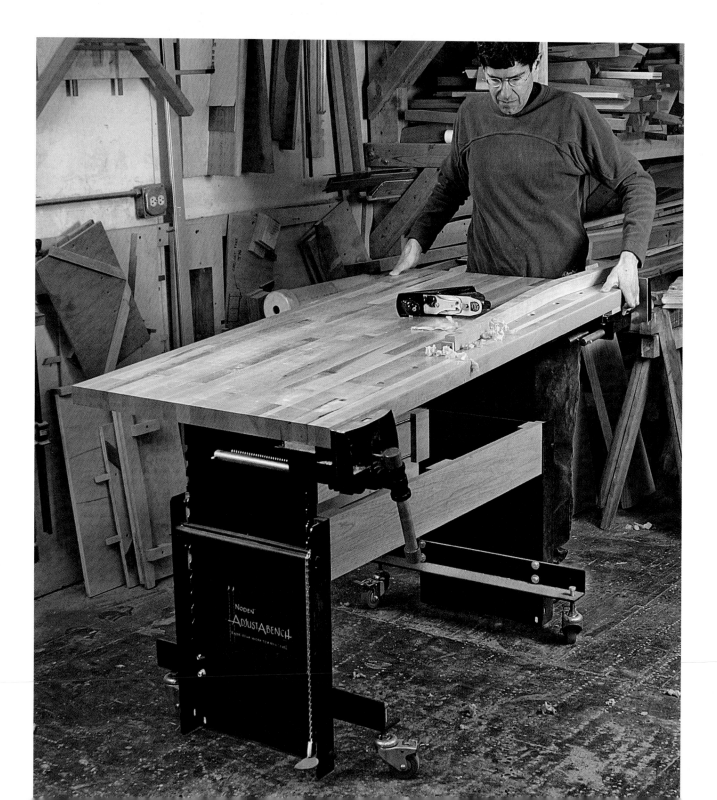

Liftoff and landing. To raise the benchtop (see photo on the facing page), lift one end until the locking bar catches, then go around to the other end and do the same. To lower the bench (above), step on a release pedal, lift the top to disengage the stop bar, then drop to the desired height.

Suitable for planing. The Adjust-A-Bench was rigid and stationary on solid ground. On its locking casters, it moved quite a bit.

I am a big advocate of working at the proper height for specific tasks. So I was intrigued by the concept of the Noden Adjust-a-Bench™, a workbench system that can be adjusted to a variety of heights.

The Adjust-a-Bench is available as either a set of adjustable legs (you'll have to supply the top and vises) or as a complete bench, which includes the legs, a wood stretcher, and a top. We added a few accessories—benchdog holes in the top, Jorgensen vises, and locking casters. Initial assembly was straightforward and relatively easy.

The ratcheting adjustment mechanism lifts the benchtop in 1½-in. increments from roughly 28 in. to 45 in. high. This adjustable height feature proved very useful for tasks ranging from assembly work to planing to close detail work. Noden suggests using the bench as an outfeed table, but setting it to the correct height could be a very fussy operation because of the 1½-in. increments.

With the legs on the floor, the bench was rigid enough for planing tasks, even at its maximum height. Not surprisingly, though, when fitted with the casters, the bench moved quite a bit.

The top supplied by the manufacturer is essentially a 1¾-in.-thick wooden kitchen countertop, which worked well enough. It is available in three sizes: 24 in. wide to 30 in. wide and 60 in. long to 72 in. long. The one we purchased was not perfectly flat, but it was within 1/16 in., an acceptable tolerance. The Jorgensen quick-release vises are mounted on the side and end of the bench (not flush with the edge, but sticking out). They are good-quality heavy-duty vises, although small for my taste.

The adjustability of this system makes it a versatile addition to a shop. If I were buying it, I'd be inclined to purchase the base system (legs only) and add a better top and larger vises. For information about pricing, go to www.adjustabench.com.

A Convertible Clamping Workstation

GARY B. FOSTER

After working for months on my knees building a large bookcase, I decided I needed a low table in my shop for assembling large projects. Although my newly built shop is spacious at 1,040 sq. ft., I didn't want to take up room with a low table that would find only part-time use. It needed to do more. So I designed a work-station that also fulfilled a number of other shop needs, including a place to store my clamps and to glue up furniture parts. The workstation is built in two sections and can be reconfigured to accommodate its various uses.

A twist on the torsion box

The lower portion of the workstation is constructed as a tall torsion box. A plywood grid makes up its interior, consisting of five panels running widthwise and three longer panels running lengthwise. The panels, which stand on end, cross one another with crosslap joints, and they are sandwiched between two ¾-in.-thick plywood skins. Built into the lower torsion box is a web of PVC pipes that hold clamps up to 6 ft. long.

Build it from the bottom up

Begin by cutting the crosslap joints in the plywood panels with a ¾-in. plywood router

Lower section: Mobile assembly table

The lower portion of the workstation is a tall torsion box consisting of a grid with five panels spanning the length. The ¾-in.-thick panels stand on end and cross one another with crosslap joints. The grid is sandwiched between a top and a base made of ¾-in.-thick plywood, which is attached with glue and 2½-in.-long drywall screws.

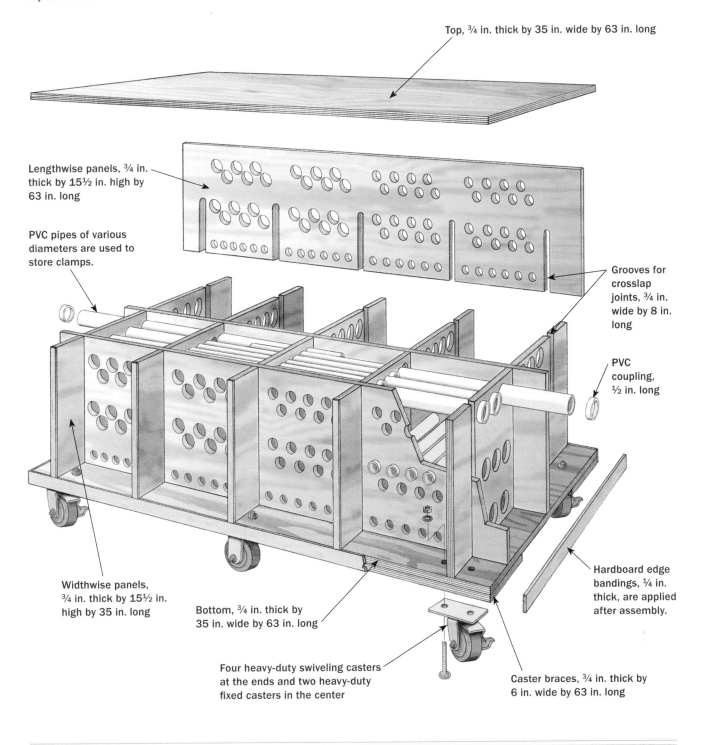

Top, ¾ in. thick by 35 in. wide by 63 in. long

Lengthwise panels, ¾ in. thick by 15½ in. high by 63 in. long

PVC pipes of various diameters are used to store clamps.

Grooves for crosslap joints, ¾ in. wide by 8 in. long

PVC coupling, ½ in. long

Widthwise panels, ¾ in. thick by 15½ in. high by 35 in. long

Bottom, ¾ in. thick by 35 in. wide by 63 in. long

Four heavy-duty swiveling casters at the ends and two heavy-duty fixed casters in the center

Caster braces, ¾ in. thick by 6 in. wide by 63 in. long

Hardboard edge bandings, ¼ in. thick, are applied after assembly.

Hole layout for plywood panels

PVC pipes, with diameters based on the size of the clamps they will hold, are fed through holes drilled in the plywood panels. Lay out the pipes so that those spanning the width of the table don't interfere with those running lengthwise. Prepare templates to cut matching hole patterns on each plywood panel. The end panels are mirror images of each other and are laid out with the same template. The center panels combine the layouts of the two end panels.

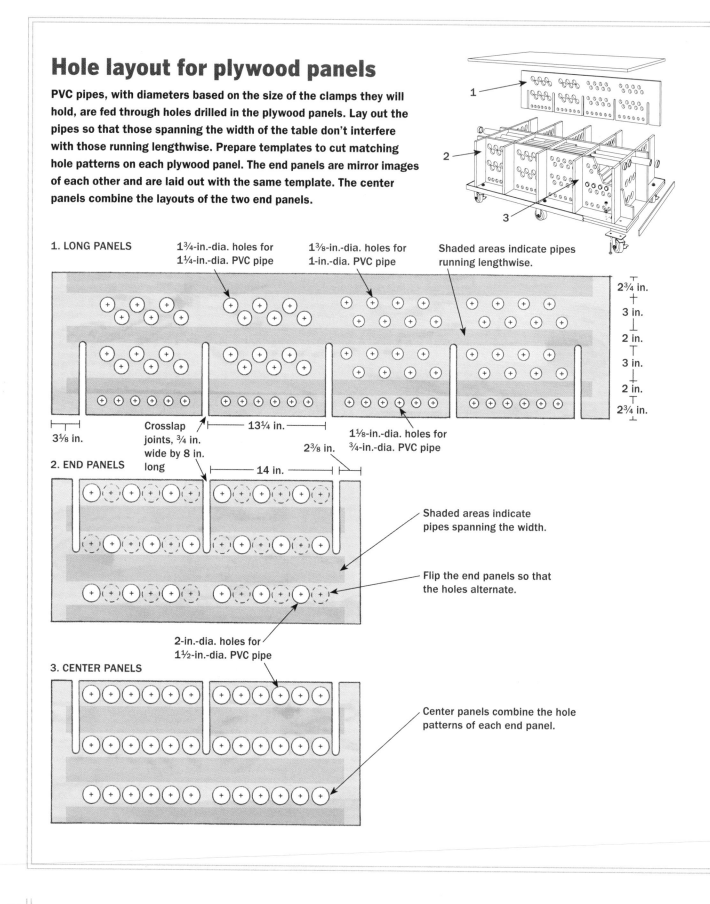

1. LONG PANELS

1¾-in.-dia. holes for 1¼-in.-dia. PVC pipe

1⅜-in.-dia. holes for 1-in.-dia. PVC pipe

Shaded areas indicate pipes running lengthwise.

2¾ in.

3 in.

2 in.

3 in.

2 in.

2¾ in.

3⅛ in.

Crosslap joints, ¾ in. wide by 8 in. long

13¼ in.

1⅛-in.-dia. holes for ¾-in.-dia. PVC pipe

2⅜ in.

2. END PANELS

14 in.

Shaded areas indicate pipes spanning the width.

Flip the end panels so that the holes alternate.

2-in.-dia. holes for 1½-in.-dia. PVC pipe

3. CENTER PANELS

Center panels combine the hole patterns of each end panel.

Prepare templates for matching holes. Transfer the center points from a paper template (top) to a ¼-in.-thick plywood template (above). Use the template to lay out each section on the final panels.

bit. This specialty bit, available from most home centers or catalog retailers, is slightly undersize to account for the actual thickness of plywood. Using this bit will make the crosslap joints fit tightly.

Next, plan and lay out the PVC piping. I chose to use several different-diameter pipes to hold the different clamps I own. The pipes extend through the torsion box's interior grid, and holes must be drilled in each plywood panel in the same location so that the pipes can feed through properly. I created a template to locate and drill pilot holes in each of the interior panels, and then bored each hole with an appropriately sized holesaw.

After the plywood panels are prepared, begin assembling the torsion box. It must be constructed on a flat surface and upside down. Fit together the plywood grid and attach the bottom skin with glue and 2½-in.-long gold drywall screws.

While the box is upside down, attach six heavy-duty casters with carriage bolts. I applied an extra strip of plywood between the bottom panel and the casters to provide extra strength for carrying the weight of the table as it's rolled around the shop. I used 6-in. casters rated at 700 lb., purchased from an industrial-supply store. The four corner casters spin and the two center casters are fixed, making the workstation easy to maneuver around the shop.

Plumb the table for clamp storage

Flip over the torsion box to install the piping and the top skin. Install the lowest row of piping first and work your way up the table. To secure the pipes, purchase PVC couplings from any plumbing-supply store and cut the couplings into ½-in. rings on a bandsaw while holding them with locking pliers to keep them straight.

The pipes spanning the width of the table are 1 in. longer than the width of the torsion

Make clamp holder out of PVC pipe and PVC couplings

PVC pipe holds clamp.

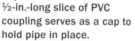

½-in.-long slice of PVC coupling serves as a cap to hold pipe in place.

Install the pipes. Use PVC glue to attach the rings to the pipes. Work from the lowest row to the top.

Space-saving clamp storage. Offset the holes for the PVC pipes to maximize storage space. If clamps interfere with each other, you can insert some from the other side.

box and project ½ in. at both ends. Glue a ring over one end of the PVC pipe and feed it through the plywood grid. The pipe should extend ½ in. from the other side of the table. Cap that end with a ½-in. ring.

The pipes spanning the length of the table are installed from both sides of the table but are accessible only from one end. These pipes should be cut roughly 10 in. shorter than the length of the torsion box. Cap off one end of the pipe with a ½-in. ring and feed it through the table.

Clamp table makes glue-up easy

The upper section of the table stacks on top of the lower section and is designed to support clamps when assembling furniture parts. It also is constructed as a tall torsion box with panels that lock together with crosslap joints. However, this torsion box is not glued, so it can be reconfigured to hold clamps in different arrangements. Use a standard ¾-in. straight router bit when cutting the crosslap joints so that the plywood panels have wiggle room for assembly and disassembly. Although most of the table is finished with oil-based polyurethane, these boards should be finished with a water-based polyurethane and waxed regularly to keep them from sticking.

To secure the upper section to the bottom, I installed four ⅜-in. wood dowels in each corner of the upper torsion box and drilled matching holes in the top surface of the lower table assembly.

Grooves hold clamps level

On the top edge of the plywood panels, grooves are cut at regular intervals and sized to hold clamps. I've designed my table to hold Bessey® K-body clamps and Jorgensen I-bar clamps, so the grooves cut in the top edge of the plywood panels are sized for those. Grooves can be cut for clamps from any manufacturer. Size them so that the width of the groove is equal to the width of the clamp, and the height of the groove is ⅛ in. shallower than the height of the clamp. As a result, the clamp will sit proud by ⅛ in. and keep a workpiece out of contact with the table during glue-up.

Gluing up some furniture parts, such as frame-and-panel doors, requires clamping in two directions to apply pressure on four edges. To accommodate two-directional clamping, grooves spanning the width of the table can be cut twice as deep as those along the length of the table. This way, the two clamps won't come in contact with each other when they cross.

Top off the table with a sheet of melamine

The upper section also can be used as a work surface by laying a sheet of ¾-in.-thick melamine on top of the plywood grid. With the top on, the table is level with my workbench and tablesaw, so it is useful as an infeed or outfeed support.

Again, install four wood dowels on the underside of the top sheet. Matching holes are drilled into the top edge of the upper torsion box and keep the work surface locked in position.

Upper section: Knockdown table doubles as clamping grid

The upper section of the workstation is a torsion box consisting of tall plywood panels connected by crosslap joints. The panels are not glued together, so they can be reconfigured for different clamping arrangements. Grooves in the top edges of the panels support clamps during glue-up. In one configuration, grooves in the lengthwise panels are twice as deep as those in the widthwise panels. This allows clamps to be arranged front to back and side to side without interference. With the top panel in place, the workstation can be used as a large work surface.

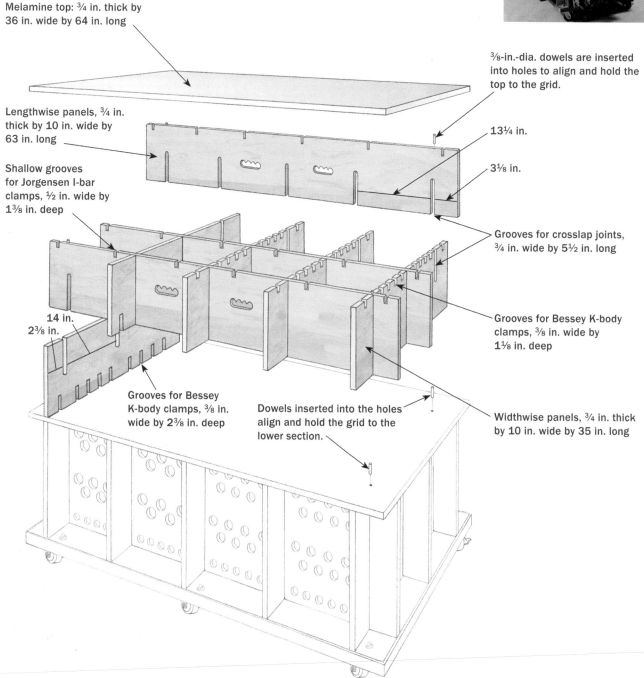

Melamine top: ¾ in. thick by 36 in. wide by 64 in. long

Lengthwise panels, ¾ in. thick by 10 in. wide by 63 in. long

Shallow grooves for Jorgensen I-bar clamps, ½ in. wide by 1⅜ in. deep

14 in.

2⅜ in.

Grooves for Bessey K-body clamps, ⅜ in. wide by 2⅜ in. deep

Dowels inserted into the holes align and hold the grid to the lower section.

⅜-in.-dia. dowels are inserted into holes to align and hold the top to the grid.

13¼ in.

3⅛ in.

Grooves for crosslap joints, ¾ in. wide by 5½ in. long

Grooves for Bessey K-body clamps, ⅜ in. wide by 1⅛ in. deep

Widthwise panels, ¾ in. thick by 10 in. wide by 35 in. long

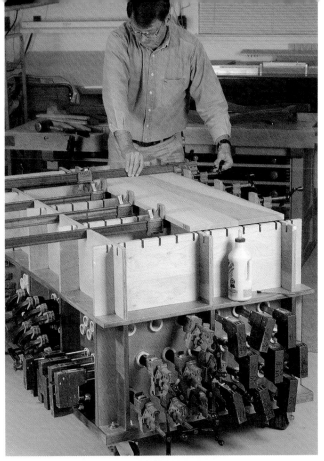

Setup for large panels. Crosslap joints make for easy assembly and disassembly of plywood grid. Bar clamps rest in grooves cut into the top edges of the plywood grid. The bars extend ⅛ in. above the plywood edge to provide clearance during glue-up.

Setup for panel doors. Reconfigure the grid for two-directional clamping. Grooves of various depths cut into the five short plywood panels allow the grid to be arranged so that clamps situated front to back can sit below those running side to side.

A Low
Assembly
Bench

BILL NYBERG

My father learned woodworking in Sweden, and when he came to this country, he got a job building reproduction early American furniture. The shop had been in operation since the late 1700s, and like those who worked before him, my father was assigned a huge bench with many drawers. He stored his tools and ate his lunch at the bench, but much of his actual work took place nearby on a low table he called "the platform."

When I inherited his big bench, I also found myself doing most of my work at a low platform improvised from sawhorses and planks. I have bad shoulders and the occasional sore back, so using a full-height bench is difficult and unproductive. I needed a bench that suited the way I really work, so I built a low platform that incorporates some features of a traditional full-size bench.

A clamping machine

My low platform bench is made for clamping (see the photos on the facing page). The edges overhang enough for clamps to get a good grip anywhere along the length of the bench. A 4-in.-wide space down the middle increases the clamping options.

This platform bench has four tail vises made from Pony No. 53 double-pipe clamps, which can be used by themselves or in combination with a row of dogs on the centerline between the screws, as the drawing on p. 162

shows. Unlike most bench arrangements, with a single row of dogs along one edge, this one doesn't twist or buckle the piece. I can use each vise singly or with the others because the pipes are pinned into the bench-tops at each end with ¼-in. by 2-in. roll pins. Without the pins, the pipes would slide through the bench when tightening one end.

Rather than using traditional square bench dogs, I bored ¾-in. holes for a variety of manufactured dog fixtures or shopmade dowel dogs (see the drawing on p. 162).

Building the benchtops

The bench is made from eight straight, clear 8-ft. 2×4s that I had kept in the shop for a few months to dry. I jointed the edges and then ran each of the boards through the planer until the radiused corners were square.

Building the legs and base according to the dimensions on the drawing is straightforward. The only point to note is the dovetail connecting the beams to the legs. Because of the orientation of the beams and legs, the dovetail is only 1½ in. at its widest point, but it's 3½ in. from top to bottom. I tilted the tablesaw blade to cut the tails on the beam and cut the pins on the legs in the bandsaw. Almost any method would work to join the beam to the leg; my first version of the bench used a bolted slip joint.

The pipes run through the tops

The tops are made in two sections and glued up with the pipes and vises in place. The upper sections are made of three boards and the lower section from two. I edge-glued them with alternating growth rings to eliminate cupping. I cut ⅞-in. grooves lengthwise in the top face of the bottom section to accommodate the pipes.

The tops are held to each beam with a single lag screw, which allows seasonal move-

Make clamping easy. Two vises that can be adjusted independently hold even irregular shapes securely (top). The open space at the center of the bench allows clamping pressure to be applied anywhere (above).

A low bench made for clamping

This bench is 24 in. high, a convenient height for working on many projects. The benchtops are 42½ in. long, which gives more than 4 ft. between the jaws. At about 70 lbs., the bench is light enough to move around yet heavy enough for stability.

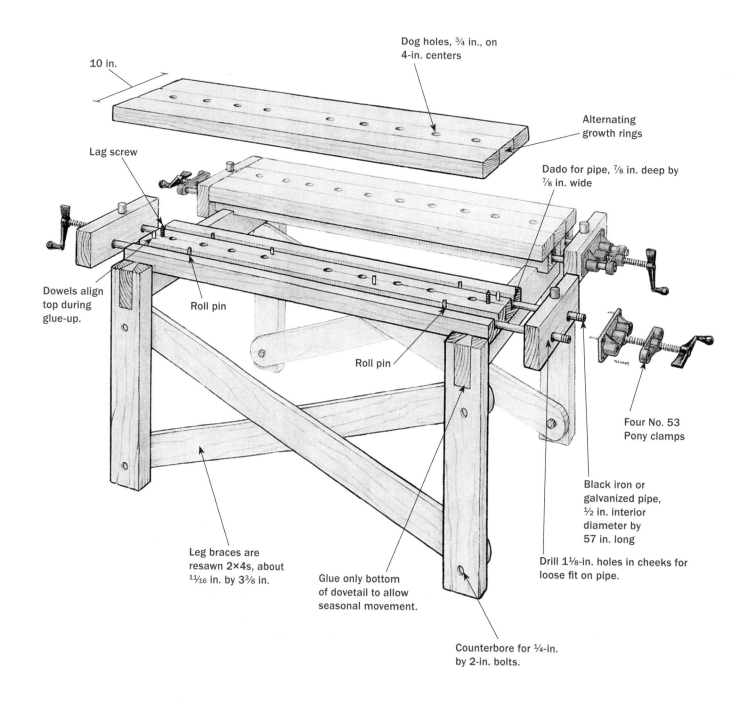

10 in.

Dog holes, ¾ in., on 4-in. centers

Alternating growth rings

Lag screw

Dado for pipe, ⅞ in. deep by ⅞ in. wide

Dowels align top during glue-up.

Roll pin

Roll pin

Four No. 53 Pony clamps

Leg braces are resawn 2×4s, about ¹¹⁄₁₆ in. by 3⅜ in.

Glue only bottom of dovetail to allow seasonal movement.

Black iron or galvanized pipe, ½ in. interior diameter by 57 in. long

Drill 1⅛-in. holes in cheeks for loose fit on pipe.

Counterbore for ¼-in. by 2-in. bolts.

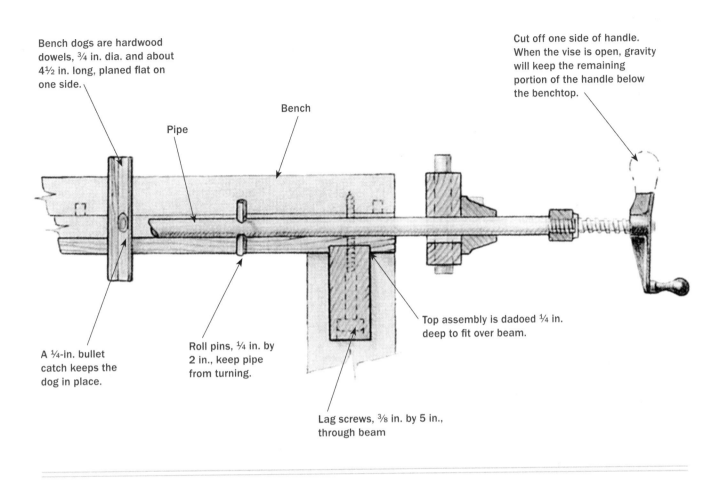

Bench dogs are hardwood dowels, ¾ in. dia. and about 4½ in. long, planed flat on one side.

Pipe

Bench

Cut off one side of handle. When the vise is open, gravity will keep the remaining portion of the handle below the benchtop.

A ¼-in. bullet catch keeps the dog in place.

Roll pins, ¼ in. by 2 in., keep pipe from turning.

Top assembly is dadoed ¼ in. deep to fit over beam.

Lag screws, ⅜ in. by 5 in., through beam

ment. To lock the tops into the base, I cut dadoes on the lower faces of the bottom sections to fit over the beams.

Assembling the double-pipe clamps

The double-pipe clamps are sold with a tail stop and a screw head. I set aside the tail-stop ends and used only the screw heads. Threading on the vise at one end of the pipe will unscrew the vise at the other end. So I had a plumber cut the threads twice as long on one end of each of the four pipes. I threaded the first vise all the way onto the end with double-long threads so that it was twice as far on the pipe as it needed to go.

By the time the second vise was in place, the first one had unscrewed itself to the correct location.

Keep ends flush when gluing

Before the pipes are installed in the grooves, I cut all the bench pieces to length. Once the tops are glued up, the pipes and vises are in the way, so it's hard to trim up ends that aren't flush. For flush ends, I aligned the pieces with dowel pins between top and bottom. I applied the glue and clamped the top and bottom sections together with the dowels in place. After the glue was dry, I drilled for the roll pins from the bottom so they wouldn't show.

Metric Equivalents

INCHES	CENTIMETERS	MILLIMETERS	INCHES	CENTIMETERS	MILLIMETERS
⅛	0.3	3	13	33.0	330
¼	0.6	6	14	35.6	356
⅜	1.0	10	15	38.1	381
½	1.3	13	16	40.6	406
⅝	1.6	16	17	43.2	432
¾	1.9	19	18	45.7	457
⅞	2.2	22	19	48.3	483
1	2.5	25	20	50.8	508
1¼	3.2	32	21	53.3	533
1½	3.8	38	22	55.9	559
1¾	4.4	44	23	58.4	584
2	5.1	51	24	61	610
2½	6.4	64	25	63.5	635
3	7.6	76	26	66.0	660
3½	8.9	89	27	68.6	686
4	10.2	102	28	71.7	717
4½	11.4	114	29	73.7	737
5	12.7	127	30	76.2	762
6	15.2	152	31	78.7	787
7	17.8	178	32	81.3	813
8	20.3	203	33	83.8	838
9	22.9	229	34	86.4	864
10	25.4	254	35	88.9	889
11	27.9	279	36	91.4	914
12	30.5	305			

Sources

From "The Essential Workbench," p. 36:
Premade Benchtop Slabs
Grizzly Industrial
800-523-4777
www.grizzly.com

Lee Valley Tools
From USA: 800-871-8158
From Canada: 800-267-8767
www.leevalley.com

Woodcraft
800-225-1153
www.woodcraft.com

Quick-Release Front Vise
Woodcraft

Veritas Twin-Screw Vise
Lee Valley Tools

Steel Benchdogs (square)
Highland Hardware
800-241-6748
www.highlandwoodworking.com

Round Benchdogs
Lee Valley Tools

From "A Bench Built to Last," p. 74
Vises, Vise Hardware, and Benchdogs
Woodcraft
800-225-1153
www.woodcraft.com

From "A Benchtop Bench," p. 143
Veneer-Press Screw, Bench Pups
Lee Valley Tools
From USA: 800-871-8158
From Canada: 800-267-8767
www.leevalley.com

Woodcraft
800-225-1153
www.woodcraft.com

Contributors

Tom Begnal is a former associate editor at *Fine Woodworking*.

Bob Belleville is a *Fine Woodworking* reader from Los Altos, California.

Mike Billick is a *Fine Woodworking* reader from Sylmar, California.

Graham Blackburn runs his own custom furniture shop and is a frequent contributor to *Fine Woodworking*.

Aurelio Bolognesi is a *Fine Woodworking* reader from Hardwick, Massachusetts.

Cecil Braeden is a woodworker near Anacortes, Washington.

Mike Dunbar is a contributing editor to *Fine Woodworking*. He and his wife, Sue, run a Windsor-chair-making school in Hampton, New Hampshire.

Joshua Finn owns a woodworking shop in High Falls, New York.

Gary B. Foster is a longtime woodworker from Folsom, California.

Chris Gochnour is a furniture maker, author, and teacher from Murray, Utah.

Garrett Hack is a *Fine Woodworking* contributor, teacher, and professional furniture maker from Thetford Center, Vermont.

Richard L. Humphreville is a furniture maker in New London, Connecticut.

Tim Janssen is a *Fine Woodworking* reader from Toronto, Ontario, Canada.

Matt Kenney is a senior editor at *Fine Woodworking*.

Phil Lowe builds and restores furniture in Beverly, Massachusetts, where he teaches classes on building traditional furniture.

Dick McDonough lives in Flint, Michigan, where he's a full-time finish carpenter and part-time woodworking teacher.

Jos Mertens is a *Fine Woodworking* reader from Venray, The Netherlands.

Jeff Miller is a furniture maker, teacher, author, and frequent *Fine Woodworking* contributor from Chicago.

Bill Nyberg is a woodworker in Marlton, New Jersey.

Timothy Sams is a former associate editor at *Fine Woodworking*.

Lon Schleining makes furniture and stairs in Capistrano Beach, California, and teaches woodworking throughout the United States.

Mark Schofield is the managing editor of *Fine Woodworking*.

Abraham Tesser is a *Fine Woodworking* reader from Athens, Georgia.

Daniel Thomas is a *Fine Woodworking* contributor from Franklin Park, Illinois.

John White is the former shop manager at *Fine Woodworking*.

Frederick Wilbur is a professional wood carver in Lovingston, Virginia. Material for this chapter was excerpted from his book, *Carving Classical Styles in Wood* (GMC Publications, 2004).

Credits

The articles in this book appeared in the following issues of Fine Woodworking:

Photos: p. i: by Asa Christiana, © The Taunton Press, Inc.; p. iii: Mark Schofield, © The Taunton Press, Inc.; p. iv: (top)photo by Mark Schofield, © The Taunton Press, Inc., (bottom) photo by Michael Pekovich, © The Taunton Press, Inc.; p. 1: William Duckworth, © The Taunton Press, Inc.

pp. 4–11: The Workbench: An Illustrated Guide by Graham Blackburn, issue 160. Drawings by Graham Blackburn, © The Taunton Press, Inc.

pp. 12–19: Forget What You Know about Workbenches by Joshua Finn, issue 202. Photos by Anissa Kapsales, © The Taunton Press, Inc.; Drawings by Jim Richey, © The Taunton Press, Inc.

pp. 20–25: Ready-Made Workbenches by Mark Schofield, issue 188. Photos by Mark Schofield, © The Taunton Press, Inc. except the photo on p. 20 by Michael Pekovich © The Taunton Press, Inc.

pp. 26–35: A Workbench Thirty Years in the Making by Garrett Hack, issue 209. Photos by Thomas McKenna, © The Taunton Press, Inc.; Drawings by David Richards, © The Taunton Press, Inc.

pp. 36–45: The Essential Workbench by Lon Schleining, issue 167. Photos by Asa Christiana, © The Taunton Press, Inc.; Drawings by Robert LaPointe, © The Taunton Press, Inc.

pp. 46–53: Tool Cabinet for a Workbench by Lon Schleining, issue 181. Photos by Asa Christiana, © The Taunton Press, Inc.; Drawings by David Richards, © The Taunton Press, Inc.

pp. 54–61: A Rock-Solid Plywood Bench by Cecil Braeden, issue 181. Photos by Mark Schofield, © The Taunton Press, Inc.; Drawings by Charles Lockhart, © The Taunton Press, Inc.

pp. 62–73: A Heavy-Duty Workbench by Mike Dunbar, issue 153. Photos by Asa Christiana, © The Taunton Press, Inc. except photo p. 64 by Michael Pekovich, © The Taunton Press, Inc.; Drawings by Robert LaPointe, © The Taunton Press, Inc.

pp. 74–80: A Bench Built to Last by Dick McDonough, issue 149. Photos by Tom Begnal, © The Taunton Press, Inc. except photos p. 80 by Erika Marks, © The Taunton Press, Inc.; Drawings by Vincent Babak, © The Taunton Press, Inc.

pp. 81–83: A Small Workbench that Works by Phil Lowe, issue 143. Photos by William Duckworth, © The Taunton Press, Inc.; Drawings by Robert LaPointe, © The Taunton Press, Inc.

pp. 84–89: A New-Fangled Workbench by John White, issue 139. Photos by Jefferson Kolle, © The Taunton Press, Inc.; Drawings by Jim Richey, © The Taunton Press, Inc.

pp. 90–97: Holding Your Work by Garrett Hack, issue 155. Photos by Michael Pekovich, © The Taunton Press, Inc.

pp. 98–105: Making Sense of Vises by Garrett Hack, issue 191. Photos by Steve Scott, © The Taunton Press, Inc.; Drawings by John Hartman, © The Taunton Press, Inc.

pp. 106–113: Thirteen Bench Vises by Matt Kenney, issue 205. Photos by Matt Kenney, © The Taunton Press, Inc.

pp. 114–117: Expand Your Workbench with Versatile Bench Hooks by Chris Gochnour, issue 174. Photos by Matthew Berger, © The Taunton Press, Inc.; Drawings by Vincent Babak, © The Taunton Press, Inc.

pp. 118–123: Installing a Cast-Iron Vise by Tom Begnal, issue 158. Photos by Michael Pekovich, © The Taunton Press, Inc.; Drawings by Melanie Powell, © The Taunton Press, Inc.

p. 124: Bar-Clamp End Vise by Mike Billick, issue 157. Drawings by Jim Richey, © The Taunton Press, Inc.

pp. 125–129: Hold Carvings Securely by Frederick Wilbur, issue 203. Photos by William Duckworth, © The Taunton Press, Inc.; Drawings by Kelly J. Dunton, © The Taunton Press, Inc.

pp. 130–137: Tune Up Your Workbench by Richard L. Humphreville, issue 156. Photos by Mark Schofield, © The Taunton Press, Inc.; Drawings by Jim Richey, © The Taunton Press, Inc.

pp. 138: Sliding Bench Jack Holds Boards on Edge at Any Height by Abraham Tesser, issue 208. Drawings by Jim Richey, © The Taunton Press, Inc.

p. 139: Pipe-Clamp Parts Make a Workbench More Versatile by Daniel Thomas, issue 207. Drawings by Jim Richey, © The Taunton Press, Inc.

p. 140: A Rolling Lift for Your Workbench by Tim Janssen, issue 198. Drawings by Jim Richey, © The Taunton Press, Inc.

p. 141: Workbench Extension Lengthens Clamping Capacity by Aurelio Bolognesi, issue 173. Drawings by Jim Richey, © The Taunton Press, Inc.

p. 142: Adjustable Support for a Workbench by Joe Mertens, issue 165. Drawings by Jim Richey, © The Taunton Press, Inc.

p. 143–148: A Benchtop Bench by Jeff Miller, issue 176. Photos by Tom Begnal, © The Taunton Press, Inc.; Drawings by Stephen Hutchings, © Hutchings and Associates

p. 149: An Adjustable-Height Worktable on Wheels by Bob Belleville, issue 205. Drawings by Jim Richey, © The Taunton Press, Inc.

pp. 150–151: A Commercially Available Adjustable Bench by Jeff Miller, issue 192. Photos by Matthew Berger, © The Taunton Press, Inc.

pp. 152–159: A Convertible Clamping Workstation by Gary B. Foster, issue 174. Photos by Matthew Berger, © The Taunton Press, Inc.; Drawings by Melanie Powell, © The Taunton Press, Inc.

p. 160–163: A Low Assembly Bench by Bill Nyberg, issue 118. Photos by Aimé Fraser, © The Taunton Press, Inc.; Drawings by Heather Lambert, © The Taunton Press, Inc.

Index

Index of Workbench Projects